MIRACLES
ALL
AROUND US

JOHN VAN DIEST, COMPILER

HARVEST HOUSE PUBLISHERS
EUGENE, OREGON

Cover by Knail

Cover photo © imagenavi / Getty Images

Published in association with the Van Diest Literary Agency, David Van Diest, Agent, PO Box 2385, Redmond, OR 97756.

For "Prisoners, and Yet..." the author's name was changed for security reasons.

MIRACLES ALL AROUND US

Copyright © 2016 by John Van Diest
Published by Harvest House Publishers
Eugene, Oregon 97402
www.harvesthousepublishers.com

Library of Congress Cataloging-in-Publication Data

Van Diest, John.
Miracles all around us / John Van Diest.
   pages cm
ISBN 978-0-7369-3803-7 (pbk.)
ISBN 978-0-7369-4233-1 (eBook)
1. Miracles. I. Title.
BT97.3.V36 2016
231.7'3—dc23

                                                                 2015025424

Printed in the United States of America

16 17 18 19 20 21 22 23 24 / BP-GL / 10 9 8 7 6 5 4 3

This book is dedicated to...

John and Ann Booth: Friends whose monumental doctoral dissertation in seminary explained how and why God used the special revelation of miracles to accomplish His purposes. John lived a life of obedience to his Savior.

Paul and Pam Johnson: Friends whose life commitment and counsel God has used to encourage many in the faith, including me.

Rod and Deanne Morris: Editors par excellence, regularly taking the scribblings of authors and making written mosaics— thank you, Rod, for using your God-given skills reflected over scores of years on hundreds of books!

Adrian Rogers: Friend whose God-given gift of preaching drew thousands to pursue the miracle of Jesus.

Bruce H. Wilkinson: Friend whose pursuit and passion to experience miracles daily is refreshing and encouraging.

CONTENTS

Miracles of Provision

Miracles of the Power of Jesus

Simple Miracles

Miracles of Healing

Everyday Miracles

PREFACE

This is my second book on miracles, and I've often found myself pondering the question, what is our fascination with miracles? I have concluded that in a world becoming increasingly more violent and uncertain, we want to believe in something—or perhaps someone—bigger and more powerful than ourselves.

If you believe in miracles—or want to—consider this poll published in *Newsweek*:

Most People Believe in Miracles

- Percentage of Americans who believe in divine miracles: 84%

- Percentage of Americans who believe in the reality of miracles described in the Bible: 79%

- Percentage of those who have personal experiences with miracles: 48%

- Percentage of those who know people who have: 63%

- Percentage of those who have prayed for a miracle: 67%

- Percentage of those who believe God or the saints cure and heal sick people who have been given no chance of survival by medical doctors: 77%

(Newsweek, May 1, 2000)

So you're not alone in your desire to believe in miracles! Here's what some well-known Christians have to say about miracles:

"Evidence from the Bible as well as personal experience convinces us that guardian angels surround us at times and protect us."

Billy Graham

"We wonder, with so many miraculous testimonies around us, how we could escape God."

Max Lucado

"Witnessing a miracle doesn't make it any more under-standable. But I have witnessed one, and I know that mir-acles don't just change the course of events, they change hearts."

David Hanson Bourke

"A true miracle is something beyond man's intellectual or scientific ability to accomplish."

Charles Ryrie

Someone once said, "Coincidence is God's way of performing a miracle anonymously" and yet, ultimately, miracles are about God. Listen to what He says to Moses: "How long will they not believe in me, despite all the miracles I have done among them?" So a word of caution, lest we too easily dismiss them: Believing in miracles—and perhaps experiencing a miracle—has a lot to do with our hearts.

Speaking about miracles, C.S. Lewis said, "Seeing depends upon where you stand." My prayer for you as you read *Miracles All Around Us* is that you will be able to truly see.

John Van Diest

Miracles of Destiny

I have been suspected of being what
is called a Fundamentalist.
That is because I never regard
any narrative as unhistorical
simply on the ground that it
includes the miraculous.

C.S. Lewis

Miracles of Destiny

Some miracles seem to have short-range benefit; others seem to have long-range importance. The destiny miracles produce consequences that set the stage for major or larger purposes. This progressive unfolding of individual miracles in the Gospel of John leads toward a greater purpose than each of the individual miracles (John 20:31).

In such cases the degree of significance of a particular miracle may be in its contribution to the larger purpose. If God's love for us is paramount—and it is—then it is no surprise that significant events and miracles are designed to express that love.

Most likely the accounts of miracle stories in this section, while individually important, have a larger "destiny" purpose for us to discover.

People Love Secrets

Dick Woodward

We want to decipher hidden codes and unlock great mysteries. We want to find buried treasure and know the inside scoop. Whisper the word "secret" and people pay attention.

Maybe that's part of the reason that a book called *The Secret* became such a national phenomenon, remaining on the *New York Times*'s bestseller list for years and selling zillions of copies. Written from a New Age-y perspective, it explores unseen dimensions of the universe and how they connect with events in our lives. It describes how our attitudes can help determine outcomes.

As psychologist Dr. Henry Cloud has put it, the enormous success of *The Secret* is intriguing on two counts. First, it shows the deep longing of so many in the world; they yearn to understand the universe and its mysteries. Second, it reveals people's hunger for principles and practices that make life work.

Like Dr. Cloud, I've followed the huge response to *The Secret*. I'm particularly intrigued by it because my pastoral ministry for the past 40 years has been centered on what I call the "Four Spiritual Secrets."

Oh, great, you say. Here comes an evangelical pastor puffin' his own ideas, trying to catch the coattails of someone else's successful book. He's probably running around the country, preaching to happy-clappy crowds, trying to climb on the "secret" bandwagon.

Not really.

I'm not running anywhere. In fact, I've been stuck pretty much in one place for decades; I'm a quadriplegic. I can't even wipe my own nose. I can't do much of anything without help, except blink, think, talk, praise God, and pray. I can't go outside and contemplate the wonders of the universe, or even tilt my head back to look at the stars. I'm stuck.

But here's the wild paradox. Even though I'm stuck, I'm free.

As I'll tell you later, my paralysis wasn't the result of a sudden accident. Over time, I gradually lost the use of my legs, my arms, my whole body. Believe me, it was weird, terrifying, and depressing. You do not want this to happen to you.

But an absolute miracle came out of this horrible situation: In direct proportion to the gradual but relentless onset of my *disability*, the *ability* of God has showed up in my experience. In my weakness, I have a richer, more dynamic, and far-reaching life than I did when I was strong.

Just what is going on here?

One thing, really—the gift of God's mind-blowing grace and His peace in spite of my circumstances.

That's why I am so motivated to write this book. (Actually, I can't "write" anything; rather, I'm talking to my computer, and when it is happy and the voice recognition software works, it takes down my thoughts. If the computer is having a bad day, then I'm stuck again.)

But in spite of my sometimes uncooperative computer, I'm overwhelmed by a passion to share the four spiritual secrets with you. They've given me supernatural peace, joy, and a miraculous sense of purpose and meaning every single day, in spite of my physical helplessness. They are the keys to a fruitful, purpose-filled journey in this world.

And though they may sound mysterious before we decode them, that's how all good secrets are. That's what I hope you'll discover in this little book. Here they are:

- I'm not, but He is.

- I can't, but He can.

- I don't want to, but He wants to.

- I didn't, but He did.

Church Bells in the Kremlin

PHILIP YANCEY

(Compiler's note: My original intention in this collection was to choose stories that were brief. I've included the two stories called "Church Bells in the Kremlin" and "Praying with the KGB" because of their uniqueness and the fact that they were miracles themselves! Unfortunately, the openness of Russia to the message of the Bible has reversed itself from those days when they seemed to welcome Christianity.)

It would be hard to overstate the chaos found in the Soviet Union, a nation about to shed its historical identity as well as its name. One day the central bank ran out of money. A few days later the second largest republic seceded. A sense of crisis pervaded everything. Doctors announced the finest hospital in Moscow might close its doors in a month—no more cash. Crime was increasing almost 50 percent per year. No one knew what the nation would look like in a year—or even six months. Who would control the nuclear weapons? Who would print the currency?

Perhaps because of the chaos, the Supreme Soviet seemed delighted to meet with our delegation. After a full day of listening to rancorous complaints from breakaway republics, an evening with nineteen foreign Christians probably seemed like a recess period.

When the letter proposing Project Christian Bridge went out in September 1991, the Supreme Soviet was the highest governing body in the nation, comparable to the U.S. Congress. By the time we arrived in Moscow, the Supreme Soviet was not doing what it was supposed to do. Five of the twelve republics had not bothered to send delegates. Most major decisions were being handed down as presidential decrees from Mikhail Gorbachev or, more significantly, from Boris Yeltsin of the Russian Republic.

We met with twenty committee chairmen and deputies in the Grand Kremlin Palace, a huge building built in the first half of the nineteenth century as a residence for the tsars. The palace, with its chandeliers, frescoed hallways, parquet floors, and decorative plaster moldings, still conveys a fine sense of grandeur. (On the way to the meeting we passed a park where stooped-over Russian women swept snow from the sidewalks with crude brooms of hand-tied straw. The contrast in an egalitarian state was stunning.)

The two groups, Supreme Soviet deputies and North American Christians, faced each other across long wooden tables. One end of the meeting room was dominated by a massive painting, in socialist realist style, of Lenin addressing a group of workers in Red Square. His face wore a severe, clench-jawed "we will right the world" expression.

Some of us could hardly believe the deputies' warm welcome. From these very offices in the Grand Kremlin Palace, other Soviet leaders had directed a campaign against God and religion over the past seventy years that was unprecedented in human history. They stripped churches, mosques, and synagogues of religious ornaments, banned religious instruction to children, and imprisoned and killed priests. The government opened forty-four antireligious museums, and published a national newspaper called *The Godless.*

Using government funds, first the League of Militant Atheists and then The Knowledge Society organized "un-evangelism" campaigns of lectures and personal witnessing with the specific aim of stamping out all religious belief. Vigilantes known as the "Godless shock brigades" went after the most stubborn believers.

Until the fall of 1990, rigorous atheism had been the official doctrine of the Soviet government. Now, exactly a year later, nineteen evangelical Christians were sitting across the table from the present leaders.

Konstantin Lubenchenko, chairman of the Supreme Soviet, introduced his side of the table, joking amiably as he came to his vice chairman, a Muslim from the republic of Azerbaijan: "He follows Muhammad, not Jesus. Who knows, someday we may find out we all serve the same God." The vice chairman, who looked like a Turkish bodybuilder squeezed into a suit two sizes too small, did not smile.

Lubenchenko is a handsome man with an expressive, strong-boned face. He wore his hair swept back from his forehead as if he had run a brush through it once, taking no time for a part. He was gregarious and witty, often interrupting his fellow deputies with jokes and repartee.

The USSR Freedom of Conscience Law, adopted in October 1990, formally abolished restrictions on religious faith. Article 5 represents the most dramatic change in policy: "The state does not fund religious organizations or activity associated with the propaganda of atheism." Government sponsorship of atheism campaigns are now illegal.

Nine months before, as a newly elected deputy, Lubenchenko had visited the United States to observe democracy in action. He happened to book a room at the Washington Sheraton the week of the National Religious Broadcasters' Convention, one of the largest gatherings of evangelical Christians. As he stood in the lobby, adrift in a foreign land whose language and customs he did not know, the wife of Alex Leonovich, an NRB delegate, overheard him speaking Russian. The Leonoviches introduced themselves to Lubenchenko. They and Mikhail Morgulis, a Russian émigré, escorted the Soviet visitor around the capital and invited him to the next day's Presidential Prayer Breakfast, where an awed Lubenchenko met President George Bush and other government leaders.

A friendship developed between Lubenchenko and American Christians, and it was mainly through these contacts that Project Christian Bridge had come about. Just one week before our visit, the Supreme Soviet elected Lubenchenko as its chairman, which guaranteed us a cordial reception.

Our meeting with the deputies opened with brief statements from both sides. Our group, well aware of the ardent antireligious policies pursued by this state government for many years, began rather tentatively. We spoke up for freedom of religion and asked for the right to distribute Bibles and broadcast religious programs without restrictions.

Lubenchenko waved these opening remarks aside, as if to say, you're preaching to the converted here. "We need the Bibles very much," he said. "Is there a way to distribute them free instead of charging, so more people can get them?" I stole a glance at the mural of Lenin, wondering what he would have thought of these developments in his motherland.

After a few more comments John Aker, a pastor from Rockford, Illinois, spoke up. In preparation for this visit, our delegation members had urged each other to avoid any tone of triumphalism. We should approach the Soviets with respect, not offending them with direct references to the failures of their country. We should be honest about the weaknesses of the United States in general and the American church in particular.

In that spirit John Aker remarked on the resurgence of the Soviet church.

"Returning home from my last visit to your country, I flew over the city of Pittsburgh just as the sun was setting to the west," he said. "It was a beautiful sunset, and I photographed it from the window of the plane. As I did so, I realized that the sun was just then rising in the Soviet Union. Going down in America, but coming up on the Soviet Union.

"Please don't be fooled by us tonight. I believe in many ways the sun seems to be going down on the church in America. We have taken too much for granted in our country and we have grown complacent. But I believe the sun is rising on the church here. Reexamine your history. Examine your spiritual legacy. And I pray you will lead your people in the light."

The deputies would have none of it. One commented wryly, "Perhaps the setting sun does not symbolize the decline of the Western church, but rather the sinking of communism in Russia!" Other deputies laughed loudly. Lubenchenko identified the speaker as a major general in charge of the Ministry of State Security.

The general continued, "In the past weeks I have been negotiating reductions in strategic nuclear weapons. I have attended many meetings with my American counterparts. The cuts we have made will make our world more secure, I believe. And yet I must say that this meeting with you Christians tonight is more important for long-term security of our nation than the meeting between our nations' presidents on eliminating nuclear weapons. Christianity can contribute much to our security as a people."

I checked the translation with the delegate beside me, who spoke Russian. Yes, I had heard right. The general really had said our meeting was more important than the START talks. A deputy from Byelorussia jumped in with warm praise for Christians who had responded so quickly to help victims of the Chernobyl disaster. Other deputies nodded assent. Another Soviet asked about the possibility of opening Christian colleges in the USSR.

Our group began to detect a pattern that would become increasingly evident throughout our trip. Whenever we tried to inject a note of realism, our Soviet hosts would cut us off. They looked on the United States, with all its problems, as a shining light of democracy; they saw the Christian church as the only hope for their demoralized citizens.

The Soviet leaders voiced a fear of total collapse and anarchy unless their society could find a way to change at the core, and for this reason they had turned to us for help. Somewhere in government files there must exist a profile of American evangelicals: They are good citizens, by and large; don't meddle too much in politics; support their leaders; and have a strong work ethic. That citizen profile is sorely lacking in the USSR. And if God must come as part of the package, well, all the better.

One deputy quizzed us on the relationship between democracy and religion. "There is a direct tie," we responded. "Democracy is based on a belief in the inherent dignity of men and women that comes from their being created in the image of God. Furthermore, we also believe that governments are given divine authority to administer justice. In that respect, you leaders are agents of God." The deputies seemed to like that idea.

In general the Soviet deputies seemed bright, earnest, and deeply concerned about the problems outside the Grand Kremlin Palace. Most were young and energetic—a good thing since they had been meeting thirteen hours straight that day—and I thought it a shame that these deputies would likely find themselves shut out of politics as the Soviet Union continued to unravel.

As the evening grew late, Lubenchenko asked one of the youngest deputies, an attractive woman in charge of cultural affairs, to sum up the new attitude toward religion. "I am impressed with how freely you can talk about your faith," she said, softly but with deep emotion. "I envy you! We have all been raised on one religion: atheism. We were trained to believe in the material world and not God. In fact, those who believed in God were frightened. A stone wall separated these people from the rest.

"Suddenly we realized that something was missing. Now religion is open to us, and we see the great eagerness of young people. I envy those young people growing up today who can study religion. This is a hard time for us, when our ideals have been destroyed. We must explore religion, which can give us a new life and a new understanding about life."

When she finished, Mikhail Morgulis, the organizer of our trip, asked if we could stand and pray. Television cameramen switched on banks of lights and roamed the room, poking their camera lenses into the faces of praying Soviet deputies, drinking in this strange sight for the benefit, and probable bewilderment, of Soviet television viewers.

On our way out we posed with our hosts for photos in the great hall, and I could not help noticing a bookstand display featuring the film *JESUS* and copies of the Bible in Russian.

What had happened to the atheistic state? The change in attitude was unfathomable. I doubted whether the U.S. Congress would have invited these same evangelical leaders to consult with them on spiritual and moral values, and I certainly couldn't remember seeing Bibles for sale in the U.S. Capitol building.

We exited the Grand Kremlin Palace, and a chorus of bells rang out in the clear October air. The Revolution had silenced all church bells until a decree from Gorbachev made it legal for them to sound again. I saw an old woman wearing a *babushka* kneeling before a cathedral in prayer, an act that would have required immense courage a few months before. The irony struck me: Within the walls of the Kremlin—officially atheistic until 1990—stand five separate gold-domed cathedrals. Is there another seat of government in all the world so crowded with churches?

A guide had pointed out a brick gate in the Kremlin wall still referred to as the "Savior Gate." It got its name from a large gilded frame mounted above the opening in the wall. Before the Revolution the frame held a painting of Jesus; since then, it has hung empty.

I looked at my watch, still set on Chicago time. It was October 31, Reformation Day. The Reformation had not penetrated the borders of Russia during the sixteenth century or any other century.

Now, in the least likely of all places, at the least likely of all times, there were unmistakable signs of spiritual awakening. "It's enough to make you a postmillennialist," muttered one member of our group.

Miracle of the Moscow Project

Doug Ross

My wife, Sandy, and I were awake early one morning in August, 1991. Lying in bed, we watched the coup in the former Soviet Union on TV as it began to unfold. I lay there waiting for Sandy to try to convince me to cancel my scheduled trip to Moscow later that week.

When she spoke it was to say, "Doug, you still have to go—your trip to Moscow is very important!"

The purpose was the Moscow International Book Fair. And my friend Jim Groen was planning a special rally to celebrate the distribution of four million Russian language New Testaments across the Soviet Union.

When I arrived in Moscow the book fair had been canceled. Several persons were dead, and a memorial for them was growing on the street where they died protesting for democracy. Boris Yeltsin was secured in the "Russian White House." And our rally was on hold.

The rally was planned to take place in the Hall of Congress inside the walls of the Kremlin. The Communist party was meeting there to deal with the crises facing the government. All we could do was pray that somehow the rally could take place.

We didn't know the future of the Communist party itself was at stake—and that it was going to be voted out of existence. That happened just in time for our rally to take place. When we received word that our rally would take place, Jim Groen, Johnny Godwin, myself, and others were assisted by Soviet soldiers in carrying boxes of New Testaments into the Hall of Congress so that each of the ten thousand people who attended that night would get a copy.

The Moscow Project was born following the Moscow International Book Fair in 1989 and our successful distribution of five thousand New Testaments at the fair. When we returned home we knew that a great door of opportunity was opening and that Christian publishers should play a vital role. What could be more important than getting Scriptures into the hands of the people in this godless country?

While at the fair in 1989 I was asked time and again by pastors, soldiers, government officials, and people on the street, "Why are you here?" I kept answering, "The Bible is the bestselling book in all the world, and we intend to make it the bestselling book in your country."

Several of us met following the book fair to discuss where to go from there. We discussed the fact that four million people lived in Moscow—why not provide a New Testament to every person living in Moscow? We presented that idea to the ECPA Board of Directors, and they gave us the green light.

Countless organizations banded together and agreed to raise 50 percent of the two-million-dollar budget as well as handle the purchasing and printing. The involvement of International Bible Society came as a result of a "chance" meeting I had with Jim Powell—then president of IBS. I suggested it would be great if they could partner with us and raise 50 percent of the budget. A few weeks later Jim called and said, "We'll do it."

Christian retailers across the country wrapped our label

around a coffee can and began to collect money. Churches took offerings. Other organizations across the world helped in a variety of ways.

During the Moscow Book Fair in 1989, we were asked to meet with several government officials. I recall that four or five of us walked over to a small building on the fairgrounds and were welcomed into a sterile conference room. One of the officials spoke: "What you are doing is illegal." This referred to our giving away New Testaments in our booth. I answered that I knew this. There was a cold silence in the room, and I asked, "But would you like to have one of our New Testaments?"

The official smiled and said yes. We had brought a copy for each man in the room. We were refused permission to distribute New Testaments at the fair in 1989. We shipped them anyway, realizing they might just disappear. They didn't, and we handed them out to lines of people throughout the fair. Dale Randolph and the World Bible Translation Center had provided the testaments for fair distribution. When the testaments were gone, we collected fifteen thousand names, and Dale shipped in New Testaments and saw to it that they were mailed within Russia to every person requesting them.

Miracles happen when those who follow Christ work together. All too often the world sees our divisions—not our common bond in Christ. Miracles require determined followers of Jesus Christ to act. We can lower a man through the roof for healing. We can simply ask to see or be healed. But we have to act. It is most unusual for a trade association like the Evangelical Christian Publishers Association to take on a project like this. I doubt it has ever happened before or since. That in itself was a miracle.

At the end of the project, after every bill was paid, we had a surplus of $10,000. We sent that money to Peter Dyneka for his ministry establishing and nurturing churches in Russia.

At least ten years later, I was listening to a speaker at our annual banquet at the Frankfurt International Book Fair when the speaker told the story of Russian Orthodox priests going from tank to tank in the streets of Moscow handing out New Testaments to the soldiers in the tanks. She credited this simple action on the part of the priests—as did others—as possibly what caused the tanks not to open fire. What she didn't know at the time was that those New Testaments were the result of the Moscow Project—provided by the very people she was speaking to.

A miracle? Yes, a project unusually blessed by God!

God at Work in Iraq

Joe Aldrich

A few months after the Gulf War a pastor from the United States got an appointment with Saddam Hussein. At the end of their meeting, Saddam asked him, "What do you want me to do for you?"

"I want you to permit the *JESUS* film to be shown on national television," he replied.

Hussein agreed. On Christmas day the *JESUS* film was broadcast nationwide to eighteen million in Iraq. How could this happen? In human terms it is unexplainable. God did it.

The People Key

BRUCE WILKINSON (REWRITTEN BY JOHN VAN DIEST)

Like so many today, I have crisscrossed the country and even continents in pursuit of Christian service assignments. One of the minor joys on those trips is an empty seat next to me, providing a choice of extra room or snooze time.

In his book *You Were Born for This*, Bruce Wilkinson tells of one such encounter. He was hoping to get some shut-eye with an empty seat next to him, but instead he felt a disappointing surge when a man boarded the plane just before the door closed. He thought maybe the newcomer would pass to another seat, but the passenger zeroed in on the seat next to Bruce. Plus, it became quite obvious that the man had had "one too many." Then he ordered another drink!

When Bruce tried to ignore him by concentrating on proof-reading his book that was about to go to press, the man remarked, "That looks like a good book" in a voice loud enough for most seated nearby to hear.

Then, out of the blue, the man asked if he was a priest. Bruce admitted he was sort of a priest. The man then shared that his best friend had been killed the previous day. He shared how difficult it was to see him dead. And how that caused him to ask the question, When I die, where will I go? He mentioned that he couldn't sleep and had prayed that God would send him a priest.

Then it dawned on Bruce that this was God's miracle—the assignment for that trip. Bruce relates the true miracle story to remind us that for "anyone, anytime, anywhere" God has arranged circumstances so that we can respond to a person in need of a miracle.

Five Fruitful Years

Paul H. Johnson

At 56 I was retired from construction and we were now strictly in the property management business, with income sufficient for retirement. I was attending a convention for Christian Business Men's Connection (CBMC) when my good friend Ted DeMoss, who was president of CBMC, said that Nancy DeMoss wanted to see me.

At this time Nancy was a fairly young widow. Her husband and our good friend, Art, had died of a heart attack while playing tennis. He was in his mid-fifties. Art had left most of his assets in a private Christian foundation. Nancy was chairman of the board, and the board members were the adult children plus Ted. The question was how best to use the millions of dollars in the fund to further the cause of Jesus Christ.

They pondered the question, often asking themselves "What would Art do?" as they discussed and planned the future activities of the foundation. They came up with a very ambitious undertaking. Art always thought big and, therefore, so did they. The plan was to publish the plan of salvation, the gospel message, clearly explained in testimonies of ten Christian celebrities, including Art. The book would have a second section telling a new believer how to take steps in developing his life with Christ. The book would be free of charge to anyone and everyone.

The question became, how do we distribute it? They thought, *If we travel around handing them out, many people will just throw the book away.* Maybe we should let people know it's available and have them ask for it—at least that would show some interest. Then they thought, *How do we let people know it is available?* They concluded, "Let's do it like Art did. We'll advertise in newspapers and magazines and on television, and we will offer it free."

As they continued, they decided to take out a full-page advertisement in every major newspaper in every city in the United States. This, indeed, was a major undertaking. It's reported that one of them said, "This will cost millions." Someone else said, "We have millions! The question is, will this work and be effective?"

The book was called *Power for Living.* They rolled out the campaign, and it indeed was very successful. The people could ask for the book by calling an 800 phone number given on the screen in the television ads and in the print ads or by filling out the coupon in the print ads. The ads all said, "No contributions are solicited, nor will any be accepted." This was to answer the skeptics who said they were building a mailing list to later offer some product for sale. That attitude had little basis because you can buy names for a mailing list for a lot less than spending the millions that they spent. Their motives were pure. They simply wanted people to know and understand how to have a personal relationship with God by simple faith.

As I said, the plan worked. Thousands of responses came in. In the back of the book was a response card for anyone who said that they prayed to receive Christ and wanted a second book that explained more about how to continue on in faith and grow as a new believer. If they sent in the card and got the second book, the campaign ended. No one got the response cards so no one was able to contact those new believers. In the follow-up material, they were urged to find a good Bible-believing church and to get involved, but it never said which one or which kind.

As the campaign ended, it was one of the most efficient ways of reaching people with the gospel. The cost per person who prayed to receive Christ was a lot less than that of the average church or missionary activities or even a Billy Graham crusade. There is nothing wrong with all the other ministries. In fact, the foundation was also helping many of them with sizable contributions. But most of them could not do a national ad campaign like *Power for Living* because they didn't have millions of dollars to do it.

Now back to why Nancy DeMoss wanted to see me. The foundation was so pleased with the success of the U.S. campaign that they wanted to take it to other countries, and she wanted me to head up that division of the foundation's ministries. She knew from Art's cousin, Ted, that I didn't have much to do in business anymore. I was excited about the opportunity and overcome and humbled with the confidence in me, but I was concerned because I had never done anything like this before. My job would be to travel to a foreign country and find nine Christian celebrities with a good, clear testimony and invite them to become involved in the project by allowing their picture and testimony to be used in the beginning of the book.

That's the way it was done in the United States, and it gave the book credibility as one started to read it. They also used these celebrities in advertisements. For instance, in the United States, one full-page ad in newspapers and magazines featured a picture of Tom Landry in the whole top half of the page. Under it was the caption, "Is football the most important thing to Tom Landry?" The copy that followed said, "While Tom Landry is one of the most successful football coaches in history with the

Dallas Cowboys, he says there is something even more important in his life than football." Then the copy described something of his faith in Christ and then announced there is a new book called *Power for Living* that tells more about what he believes. It said readers could have a copy free if they sent in the coupon or called the 800 number.

God Has Erased My Heart

Bob Griffin

I'll never forget Gikita. Uncle Gikita, we called him, in defer-
ence to his years. He was tall for a Waorani, his deeply seamed
face showing both his age and the rigors of harsh jungle life.

He would sit for hours hunkered up against one of the corner poles of our makeshift hangar in eastern Ecuador's jungle.
He felt safe there with us.

There weren't many places Gikita felt safe. He had lived in
fear all his life—fear of a revenging ambush by his own people
and fear of outsiders who would kill on the slightest provocation
as they searched the jungle for oil, orchids, monkeys, or other
treasures. But his greatest fear was of the evil spirits he could
never seem to placate.

His people were called Auca by the Quechua people, the
predominate group in the area. In the Quechua language, "auca"
means "the good people." It all depended upon which end of the
spear you stood.

Gikita trusted us. He was content to sit watching as we
worked on the planes, but he couldn't understand why we didn't
follow his tribal law and try revenge killing of our friends. Gikita

was one of the killers who had drawn worldwide attention some years earlier when he and four companions, wielding wickedly barbed wooden spears, murdered five missionaries on "Palm Beach."

For Gikita, fear slowly gave way to trust when Rachel Saint and Betty Elliott went to live in his village. But change didn't come easily. He still had vivid memories of that black day when he killed Rachel's brother and my friend, MAF pilot Nate Saint, and helped kill Betty's husband, Jim.

Rachel already had a head start in the language. Sometime before the five missionaries' martyrdom, she had found and begun working with a teenage Waorani girl, Dayuma, who, fearing for her life, had fled her village. After the death of the five missionaries, Dayuma, now a believer, was constrained to carry the message of God's love to her people. She returned to the village she had fled so long ago, not knowing if she would live or die. Two weeks later she came out of the jungle with a surprising invitation.

"We did wrong to kill the missionaries," her relatives had told Dayuma. "We want to learn to live well. We want to learn to know God. Tell the two white women we'll build a house for them. Tell them to come."

So change slowly started among the Waorani, and now Gikita had accepted Rachel's request to spend several weeks at Limoncocha, our translation center, where he leaned against the hangar post when he wasn't helping Rachel with language learning and translation. During those weeks the love and acceptance he found among us began its work, but it wasn't until after he had returned to his village that he confessed the change in his heart to Rachel. "I used to hate and kill, but now the Lord has healed my heart," he told her. Gikita, the killer who didn't have enough fingers to count the people he had murdered, had learned he could start with a clean slate as far as God was concerned.

"God has erased my heart," he said. "Now I want to live loving the Lord." Finally Gikita understood why we didn't seek revenge. Gikita had become a true Waorani.

Martin Luther: A Troubled Conscience

BILL FREEMAN

I felt myself to be reborn and to have gone through open doors into paradise."

From the day he first saw into the meaning of the statement "the just shall live by faith" until now, the reverberations of Martin Luther's revelation of justification by faith have greatly impacted the church. The dynamic of Luther's salvation experience was a combination of things: his being a sensitive and devoted Augustinian monk with a troubled conscience, his observations of the corruption of the papal system, the influence of the mystic writers upon him, and his careful examination of the precise meaning of "righteousness" and "justification" in the book of Romans.

By the time Luther saw that justification was by faith alone, and not by works, he had virtually exhausted every possible means of saving himself. He had fasted, prayed, and gone on pilgrimages. He had confessed his sins over and over again to the point that his Augustinian Vicar General, Johann von Staupitz, said to him, "Look here, if you expect Christ to forgive you, come in with something to forgive—murder, blasphemy, adultery—instead of all these minor offenses."

Luther's troubled conscience was pained over the slightest movement within him, and according to Staupitz, he seemed to thrive on his inward torment. Nevertheless, Luther's deep turmoil was preparing him to find a Christ that he had never known before. "The righteousness of God" became a revelation, not of an angry, judging God, but of the way God makes men righteous—through Christ dying on the cross, and by simple faith in that fact. Luther's own words tell the story of this far-reaching discovery:

I greatly longed to understand Paul in this letter to the Romans. Nothing stood in the way but that one expression, "the righteousness of God." I took it to mean that righteousness in which God is just and deals righteously in punishing the unjust. My inner condition was that, although an impeccable monk, I stood before God as a sinner troubled in conscience, and I had no confidence that my merit would appease Him. Therefore I did not love a righteous and angry God, but rather hated and murmured against Him. Yet I clung to the dear Paul and had a great yearning to know what he meant.

Finally, after days and nights of wrestling with the difficulty, God had mercy on me, and I saw the connection between the righteousness of God and the statement "the just shall live by his faith." Then I understand that the righteousness of God is that righteousness by which, through grace and sheer mercy, God justifies us through faith. Then I felt myself to be reborn to have gone through open doors into paradise. The whole of Scripture took on a new meaning. Before, the "righteousness of God" had filled me with hate, but now it became to me inexpressibly sweet in greater love. This passage of Paul's became to me a gate to heaven.

Compiler's Note: I've included several accounts from the history of individuals who come to faith through what seemed to be selective miracles with a special purpose. Naturally each and every conversion is a special miracle! Each story is chosen because of the diversity of their path to faith, but more importantly, the miraculous influence they contribute to the course of Christianity. While every Christian's conversion story is a miracle, like Abraham, Moses, David, and Ruth, these are Old Testament and Peter, John, and Paul are the New Testament, they had a special role in the development of God's redemptive plan—with Luther, Augustine, Calvin, Edwards, Spurgeon, and Smith in other chapters.

How I Wish He Could Have Been There

Ramez Atallah

In 1870, my great-grandfather was obliged to leave the Coptic Orthodox Church (along with his family) for hosting a Scottish Presbyterian missionary in his home for a weekly Bible study! He and the missionary reluctantly established the first evangelical church in the city of Assiut in Upper Egypt.

He had never wanted to leave the mother church, nor did the missionary intend for him to do so. Till his dying day he loved that church and yearned for the Bible to be read, taught, and lived by its people. On Wednesday, December 3, at the Coptic Cathedral, under the leadership of Pope Tawadros II, the Christians of Cairo celebrated the 150th anniversary of the Arabic Van Dyke Bible (the most commonly used Bible by Arabic-speaking Christians worldwide). The great commitment and sacrifice of foreign missionaries and Arab nationals working together in Beirut provided a remarkable translation that influenced the lives, thinking, and culture of millions of people in the region and literally shaped today's Middle Eastern Christianity.

Also in attendance were many Bible Society leaders from the

region and elsewhere. Here is how one young Christian leader described the event:

"Uncle Ramez, this is the greatest celebration I've seen in my life. I believe this is rewriting history more than any recent event. We have seen a glimpse of a great, upcoming revival. I can't thank the Lord enough…"

It was a truly festive event, as representatives of all churches in Egypt were present and their leaders shared affirming words about the importance, centrality, and impact of the Bible in the life of the Egyptian church. They also graciously affirmed the efforts of the Bible Society in making God's Word affordable and accessible in appropriate formats to all segments of society.

Many years earlier we at the Bible Society realized that the Bible was one of the most unifying factors for churches in Egypt. Last night was an incredibly encouraging affirmation of that fact. A large part of the joyous atmosphere was to see church leaders genuinely united together through their commitment to God's Word.

While more than 4,000 people were in attendance at the cathedral, countless others watched the event broadcast live on most of the Arabic Christian satellite stations, reaching millions of viewers. My great-grandfather was not there (maybe he watched the event from heaven!) but the elderly and frail pastor of the church he helped to establish made the long trip from the city of Assiut. As I hugged him after the service I was deeply moved realizing that we were celebrating the very Bible that had impacted my great-grandfather 145 years ago and had been the basis for establishing the church this pastor now serves!

We live in a time and age where everything is expected to be instant and quick results are impatiently expected. It's good to remember that God is at work for the long haul and that it may take 150 years to fully appreciate the impact of one's efforts.

I don't really expect my great-grandchildren to remember me in 145 years, but I'm grateful that I can honor my great-grandfather by having a small part in fulfilling the dreams he longed for.

Triad and the Christian Book Fair

JOHN VAN DIEST

When I first went to the Soviet Union in 1983, representing the Evangelical Christian Publishers Association, the Bible was the hottest item on the black market. Not only was it scarce, it was illegal to own one without having it registered with the KGB authorities.

If you were registered for owning a Bible, your social and occupational status was in potential jeopardy. The Soviet Union was declared an atheistic state and any vestige of Christianity was forbidden. Most of the Russian Orthodox churches were either destroyed, in ill-repair, or changed into museums. The clergy were pawns of the government. Christians were constantly hassled, persecuted, and even sent to Siberia on false charges.

The Baptist Church in Moscow was the only visible sign of religious tolerance to Christians, even though constantly visited by Russian KGB. The congregation was 98 percent women, as male attendance was dangerous occupationally.

In 1993 Christian men established the Co-Mission and challenged U.S. Christians to go to Russia. Literature was needed in Russian to enhance the programs, so commitments of $20,000 each from Multnomah Press, NavPress, and InterVarsity Press were pooled together to establish a publishing house in Moscow.

These organizations provided funds to launch and sustain Triad. At the same time, Gary Vaterlaus and his wife, who spoke Russian fluently, completed seminary, joined the vision, and agreed to lead Triad Christian Publishing in Russia.

Two years later, in 1995, I was invited to go to St. Petersburg for the Russian-Christian Book Fair. Some seventy Christian publishing companies were represented, including Triad.

After the three-year program ended, the Vaterlauses left the fledgling start-up and Anna, a native Russian with three months of publishing experience, took charge. Even with an inexperienced leader, new pressures from the Russian authorities, and financial struggles, Triad remains a thriving Christian publishing house today.

Reflecting on the early days when Bibles were scarce and the "hottest" item on the black market, it's a miracle that just twelve years later, some one hundred Christian publishers produce Bibles and Christian products for the people of that land.

Miracles of Prayer

Prayer is a powerful thing,
for God has bound and tied himself thereto.
None can believe how powerful prayer
is and what it is able to effect,
but those who have learned it by experience.

Martin Luther

Even Jesus found it necessary to pray
and make prayer an integral part of His life.
Prayer was His life.

Howard Hendricks

You do not have because you do not ask.

James 4:2 NKJV

Miracles of Prayer

While some miracles seem to just happen, there is a special cause-and-effect relationship between praying and miracles happenings. Quin Sherrer, in her classic book *Miracles Happen When You Pray*, illustrates the significance and importance of prayer that initiates miracles!

Of all the mysteries on this side of heaven, prayer is at the top of the list. Possibly the greatest weapon a Christian has today is the privilege of prayer. William Evans was right when he said, "Prayer does not need proof; it needs practice!"

Concerned about America—pray. "If My people who are called by My name will humble themselves, and pray and seek My face, and turn from their wicked ways, then will I hear from heaven, and will forgive their sin and heal their land" (2 Chronicles 7:14 NKJV). "Righteousness exalts a nation, but sin is a reproach to any people" (Proverbs 14:34 NKJV).

Concerned about life? Pray. "Trust in the LORD with all your heart, and lean not on your own understanding; in all your ways acknowledge Him, and He shall direct your paths" (Proverbs 3:5-6 NKJV).

Do you long for a miracle in your life? Pray!

Burning Bush and Holy Moses: The First Spiritual Secret

Dick Woodward

Normally I didn't pray out loud or kneel when I prayed in private. But I found myself kneeling and praying out loud, the hotel room filling and spilling with my joyful thanksgiving and praise. I knew the voice I was hearing was mine, but I had no idea where the words were coming from. I prayed on and on effortlessly; I don't know for how long.

God's presence overwhelmed me with exhilaration. My insights on issues and the boldness of my requests surprised me. I heard myself praying that I might be able to teach people in all nations and languages the truths I was discovering in the Word of God. I had no idea how He would answer that prayer, but I wasn't concerned about it because I was abandoned to Him.

I felt as if God's love was surging through me like an electric current. I had already experienced that love of God passing through me on a few occasions, as when I saw Jesus's love expressed through Mabel and me for hurting children.

But this was new. The Holy Spirit controlled me, took me beyond the sacred page, and introduced me to the Living Word. It was a meeting with God, one-on-One, and in that meeting

I was at the point where I was ready to learn the first spiritual secret God had for me.

Nothing caught on fire in that hotel room, but it was a burning bush experience. I was on holy ground. Like Moses in the Old Testament encounter with God, I realized the absolute difference between me and the God who calls Himself "I AM."

Moses had been raised in Pharaoh's palace. He was a Hebrew, but in his life of privilege as an adopted member of the royal family, he hadn't experienced the sufferings of his people. But then one day he aligned himself with the enslaved, downtrodden Hebrews and killed an abusive Egyptian taskmaster.

He was exiled to the desert, a fugitive. For forty years he herded sheep and had plenty of time to think. It was a far cry from life in Pharaoh's pagan palace, where he had but to utter a word and his desires were carried out. Now Moses was a nobody, spending his days prodding a bunch of mentally challenged sheep.

We can't imagine what happened when Moses saw God in the bush that burned with holy fire but was not consumed. All we know is Moses got the point that real power doesn't come from your place or position. Moses learned what God likes to do with somebody who has learned that he is nobody. He essentially said to Moses, "Delivering those people is not a matter of who you are, but who I am. You are not their deliverer; I am their Deliverer. You can't deliver them, but I can. You won't deliver them, but I will. And I'll deliver them through you! So go deliver them, Moses."

By application, that's what can happen when the living God shows up in our lives. What God calls us to be and do for Him is not a matter of how spiffy or talented we are. It actually has nothing to do with us, but everything to do with God and who He is.

Moses was not the Jews' deliverer. God was. We are not

whatever we need to be to do what God wants us to do. He is. The only way we'll ever do what He wants us to do is if we are a conduit for who and what He really is.

This is simple, so simple we can miss it all our lives. It's not about us and our identity, our self-esteem, our successes or worthiness or feelings of adequacy, inadequacy, or anything in between. It's about God and His identity.

When the presence of God fell upon me in that Virginia Beach hotel room, He filled me with joy and wonder. I was overwhelmed by the love of God. Like Moses, I got hold of the first spiritual secret: *I'm not, but He is.*

Somebody Was Praying

Bob Griffin

One of my pilot friends has a special reason to believe in the power of prayer.

He had climbed about fifteen hundred feet on takeoff when the Mooney's engine stopped. It didn't gasp or cough or miss. It just stopped—as if someone had shut off the gas.

He was in a bad spot. Downtown Airport is well named—nothing but tall buildings around. No place anywhere to make an emergency landing!

A quick look over his shoulder convinced him he could never make it back to the field. It was too far away. The cardinal rule in an engine failure on takeoff flashed through his mind: "Never turn back!" He turned anyway—there was no alternative.

Pray? He'd already done that before takeoff. Now he had time for no more than an anguished "HELP! LORD, HELP!" while his hands flew all over the cockpit trying everything he knew to make the engine run. Nothing worked. Silence reigned! He was going down.

But, he says, the airplane glided as though Someone's hand was underneath. He began to think he might make the airport after all, at least to belly in somewhere inside the airport boundary.

Flying on that invisible support, he crossed the fence, popped the wheels down, and touched on the big white numbers at the end of the runway. Praise the Lord!

Just that day a counselor at camp and his group of kids were praying especially for JAARS pilots and God's protection for them. Imagine their excitement when they learned how specifically God had answered their prayers. Their counselor wrote, "We just want to praise the Lord and thank Him for hearing and answering our prayers."

We do too!

Praying with the KGB

PHILIP YANCEY

*A*t the meeting in the KGB, a Gorbachev aide said in his intro-
duction, "This is an amazing scene—you are helping to start
a Christian revolution in this country, turning the thoughts of our
government toward God. You are like a stone on the waters, and the
ripples you stir up here will make it easier for others to follow." He
then introduced General Nikolai Stolyarov, a KGB vice chairman
in charge of all personnel. Among other opening remarks he said,
"Meeting with you here tonight is a plot twist that could not have
been concocted by the wildest fiction writer."

Several times in Moscow we passed the sturdy pedestal
which, until the failure of the August coup, had supported a
statue of the founder of the secret police. Toppling the statue required the use of a huge crane, and for several days the workmen
let the statue of Feliks Dzerzhinsky dangle from a steel-cable
noose high above the street, a shocking symbol of the triumph
of freedom over fear.

"The suspended statue reminded me of an oversized crucifix,
like you see in South American cities," recalled one observer.
"Only this martyr was the destroyer, not the Savior, of our people." By the time we arrived Dzerzhinsky had been dumped

unceremoniously in a park by the Moscow River, but Musco-
vites were still filing solemnly past the bare pedestal, staring at
the vacant space, shaking their heads in disbelief.

We too shook our heads in disbelief when we got a friendly
invitation to stop by the squat, hulking KGB building behind
the pedestal and sip tea with the organization's leaders. Most
of us had read dissidents' memoirs that describe in hideous detail what went on inside Lubyanka, the most famed and feared
of Moscow's many prisons. From offices above that basement
prison the KGB had overseen a vast network of prisons—several
of which accommodated over one million inmates—exposed by
Aleksandr Solzhenitsyn as "the gulag archipelago."

I felt long-buried rancor rush to the surface as we discussed
our visit to the KGB. Cautious historians put the death toll from
the camps and purges at ten to twenty million; Solzhenitsyn
reckons the figure at sixty to seventy million. I can hardly com-
prehend these numbers, but I recoil in disgust against accounts
of simple human cruelty inflicted by the KGB.

Andrei Sakharov records that agents put cockroaches in his
mail envelopes, punctured tires, smeared windows with glue,
and stole his dental bridges, glasses, and toothbrush. Solzhenitsyn writes of a friend who got a twenty-five-year prison sentence
for attending the secret reading of a novel. It is rare to meet a
Russian whose family has not been directly affected by KGB
cruelty. Now we were to sip tea with the authors of such brutish-
ness?

Some in our group, veterans of Iron Curtain days, had told
us stories of harassment by KGB informers, and we had joked
about wiretaps in our hotel, formerly the nest of the Central
Committee of the Communist party. That very day a man had
approached two of us on Red Square and asked a few harmless
questions, feigning drunkenness. We met him again in the lobby
of the KGB building, and recognizing us, he turned and ducked

into a hallway. Unlike the statue of its founder, the KGB had not simply disappeared.

And, though toppled from his pedestal outside, even Feliks Dzerzhinsky lived on inside the KGB headquarters. The room we met in had a large photo of him still hanging on the wall, along with the obligatory photo of Lenin. The wood-paneled room was arranged like a small auditorium, with long tables oriented toward a speaker's table at the end. A handful of KGB agents, their faces as blank and impassive as their movie stereotypes, stood at attention by the doorway.

An aide to Gorbachev made a few opening remarks. "This is an amazing scene," he said to us. "You are helping to start a Christian revolution in this country, turning the thoughts of our government toward God. You are like a stone on the waters, and the ripples you stir up here will make it easier for others to follow." He then introduced General Nikolai Stolyarov, a KGB vice chairman in charge of all personnel.

We nodded in gratitude, but not without doubts in that setting. What impact can a stone have on a frozen lake? In his introductory statement, General Stolyarov did his best to dispel our doubts. A young, handsome man with a strong-boned face, Stolyarov had emerged as a popular hero during the August 1991 coup. A career officer in the Air Force, at the height of the tension he had flown to Gorbachev's dacha to help rescue him. The KGB job was his "reward."

Stolyarov began with an image obviously chosen for his religious audience, one that jarred us coming from a senior KGB official. "When the coup took place it was as if the body of Christ had been taken, then resurrected. Our president was dead, and then alive again. I felt as if I had traveled all my life in the direction of that one moment. I was amazed at the peace I found at the moment of crisis, and amazed that I did not even have to use the gun at my side at such a time."

He went on for a few moments, detailing his actions against the coup. "Meeting with you here tonight," he concluded, "is a plot twist that could not have been conceived by the wildest fiction writer." Indeed. Stolyarov then opened the floor for questions.

What was his attitude toward Christians and Christian work? "Someone asked how to bring peace and quiet to the hearts of people. It is a great problem for us," the general replied. "We are united with you in working together against the powers of evil." A few looks were exchanged around the room, and eyebrows arched upward. I thought cynically of the cockroaches in Sakharov's envelopes and the humiliating strip-search of Solzhenitsyn in the prison below.

Stolyarov continued,

> We here in the USSR realize that too often we've been negligent in accepting those of the Christian faith. August 1991 shows what can happen. Seventy-four years ago we started with destruction, and now we are ending with destruction. Over the years we have destroyed many things of value. Now we have the problem what to do next? The work of the KGB is familiar to you, of course, but now we have stopped our former existence. We are reorganizing. We have given some of our former authority to another.

He proceeded along this line, following a script that could have been written by Solzhenitsyn himself. "It is our capacity for repentance, not thinking, that differentiates us from the rest of animal creation," said Solzhenitsyn, and that is the improbable word Stolyarov turned to.

> Political questions cannot be decided until there is sincere *repentance*, a return to faith by the people. That is the cross I must bear. I have been a member of the Party

for twenty years. In our study of scientific atheism we were taught that religion divides people. Now we see the opposite: love for God can only unite. Somehow we must learn to put together the missionary role—absolutely critical for us now—and also learn from Marx that man can't appreciate life if he is hungry.

Suddenly our heads were spinning. Was that "missionary role" he said? Where did he learn the phrase "bear a cross"? And the other word—"repentance"? Did the translator get that right? What to make of this never-never land in which the KGB general now sounds like a seminarian? I glanced at Peter and Anita Deyneka, banned from the country for thirteen years, their visas always rejected because of their Christian activity, now munching cookies in the KGB headquarters. Hearing Stolyarov's words in the original Russian, and then in the English translation, they still could hardly believe them.

Stolyarov could not get off the hook so easily. Joel Nederhood, a refined gentleman who makes radio and television broadcasts for the Christian Reformed Church, stood with a question. "General, many of us have even lost family members there." His boldness caught some of his colleagues off guard, and the tension in the room noticeably thickened. "Your agency, of course, is responsible for overseeing the prisons. How do you respond to the past, and what changes have you put in place now?"

"I have spoken of repentance," Stolyarov replied in measured tones. "This is an essential step. You probably know of Abuladze's film by that title. There can be no perestroika apart from repentance. The time has come to repentance. The time has come to repent of that past. We have broken the Ten Commandments and for this we pay today."

I had seen *Repentance* by Tengiz Abuladze, and Stolyarov's

allusion to it was no less startling than if he had cited Joseph McCarthy. The movie depicts false denunciations, forced imprisonment, the razing of churches—the very acts that had earned the KGB its reputation for cruelty in general and persecution of religion in particular. In Stalin's era an estimated forty-two thousand priests lost their lives. Ninety-eight of every one hundred Orthodox churches were shuttered. *Repentance* portrays these atrocities from the vantage point of one provincial town.

In the film's most tender scene, women of the village rummage through the mud of a lumberyard inspecting a shipment of logs that has just floated down the river. They are searching for messages from their imprisoned husbands who cut these logs in a labor camp. One woman finds initials carved into the bark and, weeping, caresses the log lovingly; it is a thread of connection to a husband she cannot caress. The movie ends with a peasant woman asking directions to a church. Told that she is on the wrong street, she replies, "What good is a street that doesn't lead to a church?"

Now, sitting in the state headquarters of tyranny, in a room built just above the Lubyanka interrogation rooms, we were being told something very similar by the vice chairman of the KGB. What good is a path that doesn't lead to repentance, to the Ten Commandments, to a church?

Someone asked Stolyarov about the KGB's close relationship with the Orthodox Church. He acknowledged the problem immediately, admitting his organization had used priests as informers and had planted their own personnel in key positions. "Our government too often ended up abusing the constitution rather than protecting it," he said. "I am cutting out these activities right away."

Without warning, the meeting took a more personal turn. John Aker stood up.

General Stolyarov, I am a pastor from Rockford, Illinois. I began a career as an Army officer and was trained as an Army Intelligence Agent. I taught courses in Soviet Bloc propaganda, and participated in two high-level counter-espionage activities that involved KGB officers.

I grew up as a young boy in America very much afraid of the Soviet Union. That fear turned into distrust and finally, as an Army officer, it turned into hate.

General, I feel very privileged to be here tonight. You said something that touched a chord deep within me. I have one thing to add, though. You used the phrase, "That is the cross I must bear." I went through a time when guilt over what I had done as an Army Intelligence Agent was destroying me. I couldn't bear that guilt, and I seriously considered ending my life. That's when I realized I did not have to bear that cross forever. Jesus bore it for me.

Jesus's love for me has, in turn, given me a love for the people of the Soviet Union. This is my fourth visit in six months, and I have found them to be loving, kind, and searching people. General, I mean it sincerely when I say that as I think of you, I will pray for you.

John Aker sat down, and General Stolyarov gave a brief response. "I am deeply touched by your words. They coincide with my own feelings too. In coming to this position—even here right now with the KGB—I determined that I would never use force in dealing with people. With every power that is in me, I wish to turn the position into good."

Next, Alex Leonovich spoke. Alex had been sitting at the head table for Stolyarov. Of all the representatives selected for our delegation, Alex had the deepest personal investment in the outcome. A native of Byelorussia, he had escaped Stalin's reign of terror as a boy of seven by immigrating to the United States. After our week in Moscow he would remain behind, in hopes of returning to the town of his birth for the first time in sixty-two years.

For forty-six of those years Alex had been broadcasting Christian radio programs, often jammed, back to his homeland. He knew personally many Christians who had been tortured and persecuted for their faith. They wrote to him faithfully when his programs got through. For him, sitting next to a high official of the KGB while translating such a message of reconciliation was both bewildering and nearly incomprehensible.

Alex is a stout, grandfatherly bear of a man with gray hair and a look of kindness imprinted in the wrinkles of his face. He epitomizes the old guard of warriors who have prayed—sometimes believing and sometimes not—for more than half a century that change might come to the Soviet Union. We apparently were witnessing that very change. He spoke slowly and softly in Russian to General Stolyarov, and the Russian speakers scattered around the room translated quietly for the rest of us.

"General, many members of my family suffered because of this organization," Alex said. "I myself had to leave the land that I loved. My uncle, who was very dear to me, went to a labor camp in Siberia and never returned. I cannot possibly tell you what it means to me to hear these words tonight. My heart is full.

"General, you say that you repent. Christ taught us how to respond. On behalf of my family, on behalf of my uncle who died in the gulag, I want you to know that in the spirit of Christ I forgive you." And then Alex Leonovich, evangelist and president of Slavic Missionary Service, reached over to General Nikolai Stolyarov, vice chairman of the KGB, and the two embraced in a Russian bear hug.

Stolyarov whispered something to Alex, and not until later did we learn what he said. "Only two times in my life have I cried. Once was when I buried my mother. The other is tonight."

What was there left to do but pray? Our spokesman Mikhail Morgulis, a half-Jewish émigré whom Alex had befriended in New York and converted to Christ, rose to his feet and we all joined him. He prayed eloquently for "the thousands of our brothers and sisters who have perished," and for "the new leaders who would attempt to lead this nation down a new path." The television cameras clicked on, and cameramen vied for the best angle: Morgulis praying beneath the photo of Dzerzhinsky, the KGB guards peeking nervously about the room, General Stolyarov wiping awkwardly at his face.

After the prayer, our delegation presented Stolyarov with a Bible, a children's Bible, and a translation of the works of C.S. Lewis. "I feel like Moses," Alex said on the bus home that evening. "I have seen the promised land. I am ready for glory." He chided himself for his lack of faith. To him, and to others, our visit with the KGB seemed a sacred moment distilled from the prayers of an entire generation and poured out of a crucible of suffering.

The local photographer accompanying us had a less sanguine view. "It was all an act," he said. "They were putting on a mask for you. I can't believe it." But "Maybe I was wrong. Maybe they have changed. I don't know what to believe anymore."

The next day's *Izvestiya*, a newspaper with a circulation of eight million, featured a story with the headline "First prayer at Lubyanka." Our visit, the article said, coincided with the official day designated for the memory of those who died in the labor camps. We listened to a translation of the glowing report on our visit, and afterward one member of our group made a poignant correction. "They got all the facts right but one. There have been many prayers at Lubyanka—down in the basement. This was merely the first to make the official record."

* * * * *

Compiler's note: The very invitation to come to the Soviet Union was a miracle. I was privileged to be one of the nineteen leaders who were the guests of President Gorbachev in 1991 and was present in the KGB meeting.

Silhouette on the Screen

EXCERPTED FROM *THE POWER OF* JESUS

A traveling film team purchased space on a boat and sailed over clear, blue-green waters to an area off the coast of East Africa in historic Zanzibar to show the *JESUS* film. For two hundred years, Zanzibar was the gateway for slave trade to the Middle East and Asia. Today, the people of Zanzibar are a mix of African and Arab heritage—about 99 percent professing Muslims. And there are very few churches. For the most part, Satan's kingdom has ruled unchallenged in Zanzibar since the days of Christ.

The film team chose a site and began to set up their portable projection equipment. It was twilight, and a curious crowd began to gather. Thankfully, there was no resistance, at least not initially. When it was sufficiently dark, they began the film. The story of Jesus's life and miracles was all new, and the people were enthralled. The Word of God penetrated their hearts.

Suddenly, a strange silhouette appeared on the screen, blotting out much of the image of the film. At first the team could not make it out. Then they realized it resembled the appearance of a witch doctor, a "spiritist" whom the people greatly feared. The crowd looked back to see if the witch doctor was blocking the lens. No one was there. Whatever was on the screen was not human.

The team turned off the projector, checked the lens, and re-aimed the image. When they turned the projector back on, the black silhouette was still there, blocking the picture. The team decided to continue, knowing the people could still hear the sound, the story of the gospel. As the film reels rolled, the team members got on their knees and prayed fervently, asking God to overcome the enemy, to cast out this apparent demon from their midst.

After five minutes of intense spiritual battle, the silhouette vanished just as suddenly as it had appeared. When *JESUS* concluded, many in the audience indicated that they wanted to follow Christ!

O God, Make Thy Way Plain

Oswald Chambers

One evening in late autumn, unable to concentrate, Oswald left his room and walked westward toward Queen's Park, the Sanctuary of Hollywood House. Having decided to spend the entire night in prayer, he could think of no better place to be alone than on Arthur's Seat, the highest hill overlooking Edinburgh. It took the long-legged, athletic young man less than half an hour to reach the top of the extinct volcano, which rose some eight hundred feet above the city.

It was a familiar pathway, one Oswald had followed many times along the Pipers Walk, past the clumps of heather, ascending to the top of the dry dam and then to the rocky summit. With every step, the world fell farther behind, both in sound and feeling. Chambers often sought the high places for solitude and communion with God.

In the fading light he could see the sails of ships on the wind-whipped Firth of Forth to the north. The university buildings and the surrounding Old Town lay at his feet. Wrapping a plaid around his shoulders to ward off the evening chill, Oswald walked down a few yards from the summit to a small indentation in the rock. There, shielded from the wind, he surveyed the twinkling lights of the city and poured his heart out to God.

While he prayed, the sounds below changed as evening drifted into night. The rumble of heavy wagons and trams gave way to the staccato hoofbeats of horses pulling carriages and cabs. The bells from half a dozen churches chimed eleven o'clock, accompanied by the drunken singing of some undergraduates reeling from a public house to their digs. By the stroke of midnight, quiet reigned as a fog rolled in from the firth and obscured the city.

Chambers prayed aloud, alternately thanking God and pleading with Him to make His way plain. He wanted to serve Him in art, to go where others could not hear the gospel of Jesus Christ. But the way seemed blocked, and now, perhaps, forbidden. "O God," he pleaded, "make Thy way plain to me."

As the hours wore on, his soul cried out in anguished silence. Sometime during the night, according to Chambers's account, he heard a voice that actually spoke these words: "I want you in My service—but I can do without you."

Was that the guidance he sought? Was this the answer to his struggle? Suddenly the call to the ministry seemed so clear. He was ready to obey, but how? What should he do? It was a call with no more guidance than he possessed before.

What Counts Most?

BERNIE MAY

It was 10:22 a.m., Tuesday, January 22, and the weather was sour. I was over Sioux City, Iowa, in a Cessna 182 amphibian flying from Iquitos, Peru, to Winnipeg, Canada. It was snowing and the temperature was twenty degrees below zero.

The radios were on the blink, the engine was running rough, and the landing gear had frozen. One wheel was up, one wheel down. I was running out of airspeed, altitude, and experience all at once. Even though I was praying up there in the cockpit, I wished there was some way to let others know of my situation. I desperately needed their prayers too.

As I let down through the snow to the Sioux City airport, I realized I was going to have to land in a thirty-knots quartering headwind. But it was God's provision. The wind was strong enough to allow me to land on one wheel and keep the other side in the air until I slowed and settled to the runway without a scratch. The asbestos-suited firemen didn't have to lift a finger. The plane was towed into a hangar, serviced, and the next day I completed the trip to Canada.

The following week I was in Colmar, Pennsylvania, and met a Mrs. Ziegler. She surprised me by saying that I was one of the missionaries she often prayed for.

"In fact," she said, "last Tuesday morning I was to attend a women's prayer meeting, but it was canceled because of a snowstorm. So I stayed home and spent half an hour in prayer just for you." We compared Sioux City time with Colmar time. At 10:22 a.m., this dear friend was kneeling before the throne, interceding for me. Right on!

On my office is a planning chart. It lists the men assigned to JAARS operations in thirteen countries. Recently I've been taking a few minutes each day and praying for some of the people on that list. Each day I take a country, such as Bolivia, and spend a few minutes visualizing each man and his family. I try to visualize their circumstances, and then I ask God to meet their needs.

I do a lot of things for JAARS: planning, scheduling, managing, traveling, speaking, directing. Yet I'm slowly realizing that it is what God does for us that counts most. Who knows, but perhaps those few minutes that I spend in prayer each day are my most significant contribution.

It's not an idle statement: "More things are wrought by prayer than this world dreams of."

Prayer That Moves a Minivan

Tim Jennings

My mother is a home health nurse, and she often finds herself alone in rather frightening parts of town. One afternoon in 2001, after finishing with her first patient of the day, she had an incredible experience that revealed to her that she was never alone. She was backing down a long, narrow driveway with large rocks along the side when she backed off the driveway and got stuck on the rocks. She was driving on old Dodge minivan, and no matter what she tried it wouldn't move. She was very concerned because her next patient was a diabetic who couldn't care for himself. This is her accounting of what happened next.

"Lord, please help me. I need to get to my next patient, who is diabetic. He has no one to take his blood sugar or give him insulin and he cannot do this himself." No sooner was the prayer out of my mouth than four men appeared from behind the van and asked if they could help me. I said, "I cannot get this van to move off the rocks," and explained that I really needed to get to my diabetic patient. Each man turned and went to one of the four corners of the van and simply picked it up, as if it was a light toy, and set it down in the driveway off the rocks. I asked if they would back it onto the street for me, and one of them did.

I thanked them and asked if I could pay them, but they were gone. I did not see them walk away. I did not see them walking on the street behind me or in front of me. They simply disappeared.

The Prayers of an Old Lady

BENIAMIN LUP

I entered the house of an elderly Christian lady. She was sitting with her face toward the window. She said, "The Lord sent you here!" She said she was seventy-five years old and had prayed for thirty-seven years that someone would bring the gospel to the obscure town of Domasnea, Romania. She was the only known believer in the town.

We scheduled the showing of the *JESUS* film for April 1, 1994. When they went to the hall to get ready for the showing, it was locked. The local priest who was staunchly opposed to the showing and was also a member of the town council had locked the door, taken the keys, welded the doors, and left town! The mayor said that if he had the keys he would open it.

It was a very cold evening and it looked like the showing would be canceled. A neighbor next to the hall said she would supply the electricity for the projector in order to show it outdoors. Another neighbor gave two bedsheets for the screen. They hung the sheets on the side of the neighbor's house. They did not know if people would come, but when darkness arrived so did over three hundred people. They were captivated by the contents of the movie!

That same evening the witch in town—one people paid for her services—had put a curse on another lady. The cure in such cases was to have the witch take an item from the cursed lady to the cemetery while she was asleep in the witch's house! That evening the witch left for the cemetery and "happened" to pass by the place where the film was being shown.

She stopped and watched the whole film showing. During the crucifixion scene, some people reacted against the soldiers in the film—even cursing at them! That village had been kept in darkness by the priest for years. The witch never went to the cemetery, but returned to her home, returned the money to the lady and said, "I'll never do that again. Tonight Jesus came to our village. I saw Him dying in my place!"

Six months later the witch was baptized. When asked what had led her to Christ she said, "It was not your message, but the message from the film that Jesus died in my place."

Many of the village became Christians. Today there is a new, growing church in that village. And a new church building was dedicated two years ago.

An Ax Head Swim?

Bob Griffin

The JAARS DC-3 was peacefully motoring along above the jungle in Bolivia when the right engine developed a bad case of the shakes. Without warning it abruptly vomited oil all over itself.

That's nasty news anywhere, let alone when you're flying over a jillion telephone poles camouflaged to look like trees. The crew was experienced. Through systematically flipping switches, they shut the bummer down and coasted with a single-engine to the closest airstrip, a place called Trinidad, which is nothing more than a wide spot in the jungle. No hangar. No mechanic shop. Just a grass runway and a few shacks.

The next day, stripped of its cowling, the naked engine divulged the source of the bad vibes. Five of the sixteen studs holding the bottom cylinder to the engine case were broken. No major problem. Procedure simply called for replacement of all the studs and installation of a new cylinder. Experience called for such spare parts to be carried along and stowed in the aft baggage bin. Sure enough, all the necessities were there, including basic tools.

That was the good news.

The bad news: While two of the studs came out easily, three were broken flush and refused to budge. They seemed welded into their holes.

All day the crew struggled. Finally, tired, sweaty, and frustrated, they were ready to throw in the towel. They needed more than wrenches. They needed special tools. But that was impossible in the middle of the jungle, five hundred miles from the nearest help.

Lord, what do we do now? the discouraged pilot wondered as he sat resting under the shade of a nearby tree. Then he remembered an Old Testament story from his Bible reading. If God could make an iron ax head swim for Elisha, surely He could make these studs swim right out of their holes.

Foolishness? Absolutely. You don't find a section for miracles in any mechanics manual. The coefficient of friction, plus the inability to apply torque, leaves more than reasonable doubt for the swimming party of broken studs.

The crew gathered around the engine and prayed. Then, when the wrench was applied, those stubborn studs swam out. It worked. Contrary to all logic, it worked! By day's end the new cylinder was bolted in place, the engine cranked for a test, and the next day the plane was back in the air.

Yes, the prayer of faith can still make ax heads swim. Foolishness? Ask the crew of the DC-3.

Rice Paddies Make Terrible Airstrips

Bob Griffin

Pilots, including me, delight in bugging their non-aviator friends with corny aviation jokes. One of my favorites is to ask—with a straight face—if the hapless victim knows what the propeller on the airplane is for. Many, anxious to show off their knowledge of aerodynamics, struggle for an answer. The prop provides thrust, some say, or it drags the plane through the air. Some think the propeller makes wind over the wing to make it lift. We guffaw with delight.

"Nope, that's a good try, but that's not it. You're trying to be too technical." And then with a sly grin we lay it on them.

"The propeller is on the airplane to keep the pilot cool." When their eyebrows go up in disbelief, we pause and dramatically add, "If you don't believe it, you should see the poor pilot sweat when it stops." It's always a good laugh.

But there are times when it isn't funny. I'll never forget one of those times.

I'd been hopping like a grasshopper from one tiny up-the-side-of-the-mountain airstrip to another for three or four days in the northern mountains of the Philippines, too busy to think much about the consequences of an engine failure. Anyway, it's best not to let your mind dwell on that too much. A forced landing in those mountains is something to really make the pilot sweat. There's absolutely no place to go except to crash-land up the side of some slope and hope for the best.

With the project completed, I stopped by our northern center late one afternoon for fuel and a passenger and then headed 175 miles south to Manila, where Louise and our four daughters were waiting to begin a week's holiday. En route over a broad, beautiful valley, the engine suddenly went *kachunk*—a loud, scary-sounding *kachunk*—and smoke filled the cockpit. Almost immediately the oil pressure needle began flicking to a rapid descent toward zero. I learned later that the engine's lifeblood was gushing from a horrible wound in its side and spreading an oily film all over the airplane's belly. Below, there was nothing but muddy, water-filled rice paddies. Rice paddies make terrible landing strips.

But just over the nose appeared the valley town of Cabanatuan, where some dear Filipino, bless him, had begun a small housing development. There, on the north edge of town in geometric precision, were streets all laid out and graded, but nothing else. No light poles, no electric lines, no houses, nothing but a grid of lovely places to land my sick airplane. The developer didn't know it, but he had prepared an emergency landing strip just for me, exactly where and when I needed it.

That forced landing was a no-sweat operation even without the cooling fan up front—well, almost. True, I had the security of a place to land right under me. But without power, the approach to a landing has to be just right. There is no such thing as a second chance. Goof this one up, and I'd make a muddy splash in the rice paddy. But I did it! I made a perfect landing.

Three days later, the damaged engine exchanged for one newly overhauled, I flew the plane out, rejoicing that even though the engine failure had put the kibosh on our family vacation,

I had seen God again answer a specific prayer I had prayed for many years.

Lord, I had asked countless times while we inspected our aircraft, *give us eyes to see the problems so we can correct them. And Lord, knowing we can't see into the bowels of the engine, please permit engine problems to occur only in such a place that we can effect a safe landing.*

Naive? I don't think so. That prayer has been answered at least a dozen times, either for me or the colleagues on my crew. I am convinced it wasn't just happenstance that the prop didn't stop three or four days earlier when I would have really sweated with no choice but to crash-land amidst the rocks and trees on the side of some mountain. That day I learned it's not the propeller that keeps the pilot cool. It's prayer.

Aurelius Augustine: A Sinful Life

Bill Freeman

Augustine's life and ministry has left an indelible mark on the history of the church. He was an able defender of the Christian faith whose writings were deeply founded in personal experience.

Augustine was a son of the many prayers of his mother, Monica. She had the greatest impact upon his life in the years leading up to his dynamic experience of salvation. Part of that impact was her relation to Augustine of a vision that revealed he would one day be saved in answer to her prayers.

As a youth Augustine lived a checkered life. He dabbled in rhetoric, theater, philosophy, and heresy, at the same time he lived a sinful life with one mistress and then another. The inability within himself to give up his lust and sinful way of life eventually became the focal point of his struggle that led him to find Christ.

In her deep desire to win Augustine to the Lord, his mother would often entreat others with tears to plead with him. One such person was a faithful bishop, who declined because he felt Augustine was not yet in a state to hear the gospel. The bishop left her with these words: "Leave him there, and only pray to God for him; he will discover by reading what is his error, and how great his impiety. Go, live so; it cannot be that the son of those tears will perish."

While his mother was praying for him, Augustine was coming under the powerful preaching of Ambrose in Milan. Concerning him, Augustine said, "I was led to him unknowingly by God, that I might knowingly be led to God by him." The main verse that was on the lips of Ambrose in those days was 2 Corinthians 3:6, "The letter kills, but the Spirit gives life" (NKJV). This made a deep impression upon Augustine.

At this juncture in his life, he was also deeply touched by hearing the testimony of Victorinus, a teacher of rhetoric Augustine admired. Victorinus had found Christ and taken a bold stand to forsake the ways of the world. A friend of Augustine's related Victorinus's testimony to him, upon which Augustine said,

I was on fire to imitate him. By his choice to give up his school of rhetoric for the sake of Christ, he seemed to me not only courageous but actually fortunate, because it gave him opportunity to devote himself wholly to You. I longed for the same opportunity, but I was bound, not with the iron of another's chains, but by my own iron will. The enemy held my will, and made a chain of it and bound me. For from a perverse will lust was born, and by giving into lust a habit was created, and when this habit was not resisted, it became necessity. These were like links hanging one on another—which is why I have called it a chain—and their hard bondage held me.

It was in this condition of sinful gloom that God came to Augustine through His Word to set him free. His own words, from his confessions to the Lord, bear clear testimony to the grace of God operating in and over him to lead him to the dynamic answer to all of his mother's tears and prayers.

Miracles of Protection

The angels...regard our safety,
undertake our defense, direct our ways,
and exercise a constant solitude
that no evil befalls us.

John Calvin

Miracles of Protection

When the apostle John was exiled to the island of Patmos in the Aegean Sea, he had a panoramic vision of the future recorded in the book of Revelation. Part of the vision included millions of angels worshiping Jesus Christ! (Revelation 5:11-14).

Among the many duties of angels is to protect. David the psalmist specifically says that angels protect God's people (Psalm 91:11). Stories of angels' protection are abundant, possibly most of them beyond our awareness. This ought to provide assurance and comfort for those who are on the "front line" of Christian witness, particularly when the adversary the devil makes his primary focus to hurt Christians.

"He will cover you with his feathers. He will shelter you with his wings. His faithful promises are your armor and protection" (Psalm 91:4).

Captive in Iran

Maryam Rostampour and Marziyeh Amirizadeh

Maryam and Marziyeh seemed to be typical college-age gals, but their story was anything but typical. They lived together as Jesus's followers and used their small apartment as a combination residence and warehouse for Christian materials. While Muslim in name and dress, they knew that converting to Christianity was punishable by death! For three years they had spent all their time sharing the gospel and distributing New Testaments—about twenty thousand during that time.

The authorities finally arrested them and took them to the notorious prison called Evin, originally built in Iran for those who opposed the shah years before. They were charged with "advertising and promoting Christianity." Evin prison was their "home" for 250 days.

After experiencing the horrors of Evin prison, they began to sense why God had allowed them to be at Evin. They decided to share their faith inside the prison, while constantly confronted by guards with the threat of torture and death. Even up to this point in their story, the fact that they were still alive was a miracle. The following are two miracle stories of the girls while in prison.

"A New Prisoner" by Maryam and Marziyeh

The next morning I woke up with a terrible pain in my abdomen. Some kidney problems I'd had in the past were flaring up again, thanks to the stress, bad food, and cold floors. I called for the guard to unlock our door so I could go to the toilet, but my cries went unanswered. By the time the guards came to open the cells for the morning, I had wet myself. I feared I might be losing control altogether and hoped the problem would not be with me from then on. When the door was unlocked at last, I washed my clothes in the sink and wore my coat while they dried.

With the New Year's holiday approaching, most of the prisoners were called and set free that morning, leaving only a few of the madams, the young addict from the night before, and Maryam and me. Though the girl still seemed dazed and uncomfortable, she was better than when she'd come in. When we asked how we could help her, she said only a few words before starting to cry. Her voice made a strange, weak, raspy sound. As we comforted her, she told us her story.

She was so addicted to meth that she had eaten some of it, which damaged her windpipe and vocal cords. Her family had tried to help her, and she was able to give it up for a while, but recently relapsed. She walked through Tehran looking for a treatment center until a kind man picked her up, gave her some money, and dropped her off at a hospital.

The hospital staff told her they weren't a detoxification center and sent her away. Walking the streets again, she had asked some policemen for some help. Instead, they beat her and drove her to Vozara.

"There's no one on earth who can help me," she said through her tears.

"The Lord will help you," I assured her. "He will not answer your cry for help with kicks and punches." Maryam and I told her a little about our lives and our Christian walk. "Trust God. Go to a church when you get out, and they will help you."

The girl's expression changed from despair to bright hope. "I will go to church, and I will never touch drugs again," she said with confidence. I held her while she cried, gave her a little money, and wished the Lord's blessing on her.

By the end of the day, every prisoner except the two of us had been called to court, and all but one had been released on bail. The pilot's wife was the last one to go, and she was sent to prison. We were left in the cell block completely alone.

We walked down the hall together, going into each cell and remembering the women we'd met there. By law, prisoners were to spend no more than three days at the Vozara Detention Center, yet we had now been there for two weeks. During that time we had witnessed to dozens of women we never would have met if the authorities had followed the usual three-day rule.

What a miracle it was that we'd been able to meet and encourage so many women. What man meant for evil, God used for His good and His glory. The people who arrested us thought we were suffering in misery. In fact, we had shared the gospel more openly behind bars than we had ever been able to do on the outside. Even two guards who had been especially rude to us apologized during that last day for the way they had acted, and they asked us to pray for them.

Now, as we entered each cell, we prayed for all the people who had been locked up there. We hoped they now had their freedom, that we had been faithful witnesses to them, and that they could continue to listen for the Spirit of Christ moving in their hearts.

Then we started thinking about the women who would be locked up there after we were gone. How could we reach out to them? There were damp places on the walls where little chunks of plaster had fallen off. Using these pieces of plaster as chalk, we wrote Bible verses and Christian messages all over the walls, and on the cell we shared a joyous celebration of faith.

"Mana" by Maryam and Marziyeh

Another prisoner, Mana, was only twenty-three, but it was hard to tell because she wore so much makeup that she looked like a clown. Though wearing makeup was against prison rules, Mana and some other prisoners wore it at night after dinner when the guards seldom came around. Despite being a naive girl, she thought deeply about many things. We teased her good-naturedly about her heavy makeup, saying we could understand how the old women would want to paint themselves, but she didn't need to do that. She listened to us patiently and wore her silly makeup just the same.

Mana was one of the inmates who scheduled telephone time for Ward 2. Unfortunately, the other inmates took advantage of her naïveté and cheated on their calls. When she figured out she had been deceived, she would throw the phone logbook on the floor and say she wouldn't do the job anymore and the office would have to get someone else. Then, after a while, she would calm down and resume her work.

One day at break, Mana said she wanted to know more about Christianity. She had wanted to ask for a while, but her telephone duties kept her too busy. "I'm not a spiritual person," she began, "but I'm very interested in Jesus and Christianity and want to know more about it.

"For many years, I've had no faith in God. Years ago, I actually tore up a copy of the Koran and set it on fire." (This is a terrible sin under Islamic law. The faithful are not to deface the Koran in any way. They're supposed to wash their hands before even touching it.) "I think God doesn't love me anymore because of what I did. I'm being punished for my lack of faith.

"I was born into a rich family. My father was a self-made man who was also involved in politics without the rest of his family knowing about it. He was killed under very suspicious circumstances. The authorities gave us his body without explaining how he died. I was young at the time, and his death was a terrible blow. We lost our fortune and our standing in the community. That's when I lost my faith and burned the Koran."

"I'm very sorry to hear about your father," I said. "But you must know that God has not abandoned you. He still loves you as much as ever. You may have lost your earthly father, but the real Father of us all is our Lord, and He would never leave you. You assume God has abandoned you for burning the Koran, when in fact it is you who are cursing yourself and abandoning Him."

Mana explained that she and her husband had been in prison for three years for stealing money from the government. Their plan was to get out on parole, retrieve the money from its hiding place, and flee the country for a life of leisure abroad. She saw it as a way to avenge her father's death.

"How can you and your husband build a happy future together based on this logic?" I asked. "I don't believe this is a path to prosperity. I don't mean to meddle in your personal life, but I beg you to start repairing your damaged relationship with the Lord by talking to Him tonight. Pray for yourself and your husband to survive these hard times by seeking the truth. He will certainly answer your prayers."

"Do you think God will ever forgive me and welcome me back?"

"Absolutely! He has already paid the price for you. Besides, I don't think you and your husband will ever prosper with this money. It won't buy you happiness. Money that belongs to others will not bring you a better life. Without God's love, all the money in the world will not make you happy."

Mana asked for prayers for herself, her husband, and their family. As I prayed, Mana hugged me tightly and started to cry.

"I feel so relaxed and peaceful," she said. "Maybe this will help with my nightmares. I have a hard time sleeping, and when I do fall asleep, I have terrible nightmares." That night, I prayed for hours that God would grant Mana solace and peace of mind and guide her in His path.

Late the next morning, Mana burst into our room so happy and excited. "Look!" she said, opening her hand to reveal a beautiful wooden cross. "I can't believe this! Last night I spoke to God for the first time and asked Him to show me the truth about Jesus Christ. Then, as I was lying in my bed this morning, a friend who knew nothing about my prayers handed me this cross and said, 'Mana, I made this at the craft center and wanted to give it to you today.'

"I can't believe God would answer my prayers so quickly with this wonderful gift! I know it's a sign and that all your words about His love are true."

Mana started coming in almost every day with exciting news about some other sign that God was listening to her. She started talking about how much she would like to have a Bible to read. She told me, "I believe what you said about seeking and finding a new path for my life. I want to see the Bible for myself and know God's message firsthand."

Though I had no way to give her a Bible, her request was another reminder of how easy it was to witness behind bars compared to the work we had done on the outside. Maryam and I didn't have to look for prospects or sneak New Testaments into their mailboxes.

We could talk to them openly, rather than hiding behind closed doors or in basements. Our fellow prisoners were hungry for the truth—desperate for it. The guilty ones felt the weight of sin for their crimes and believed Islam condemned them to punishment or death. They had lost all hope until they heard news of the true God. On the surface, the prison environment seemed to be a dead end. At the same time, the truth of Jesus, His love for sinners, and His atonement for their sins, was a miracle to these inmates, a balm for even the oldest and most painful wounds in their souls. Most of these women had lost all hope of salvation because of Islam's depiction of God as a god of retribution and revenge, a god who demanded impossible standards and had no mercy on those who failed to achieve them.

The realization that God is their Father and loves them unconditionally just as they are was a life-changing revelation. And because we were already in prison for promoting Christianity, we figured we might as well shout the good news of Jesus Christ from the rafters.

Not long afterward, as I was cleaning the floor under Mommy's bed, I discovered a long-forgotten box of what looked like trash. I asked Mrs. Mahjoob if she knew whose it was. Mrs. Mahjoob said that some prisoner who was gone must have forgotten about it and left it, and I should just throw it away. As I carried the box to the trash I looked through it, just in case. Even trash might have some value in prison. To my surprise, I found a pocket-size Gospel of Luke mixed in with the scraps and castoffs.

I quickly slipped it under the blanket on my bed. I could hardly wait to get to bed that night and start reading. When it was time for lights out, I retrieved the little book and opened the cover. On the flyleaf was an inscription and signature of Archbishop Ramsey, the former archbishop of Canterbury and leader of the Anglican Church worldwide, who had evidently given it as a gift. What a treasure and miracle it was to find it!

It's hard to describe the feeling of being able to read Scripture after being away from it for a month. Every page, every word, every letter was a blessing—a banquet for the starving soul. Maryam and I decided to share it with people who might be interested. First we loaned it to Mrs. Mahjoob. After she finished it, we gave it to Mana. When she saw it, her eyes widened in shock and amazement.

"God has answered prayers," I said, handing it over. "Now you can read a portion of the authentic Bible you've always wanted." As word got around, many, many prisoners wanted to read it. Before long, dozens of women had their first look at the true Christian Scriptures, reading the little volume signed by one of the most powerful men in the Church, who had died more than twenty years before and whose little pocket Gospel had miraculously turned up under a bed in a women's prison in the middle of Islamic Iran.

* * * * *

Compiler's note: Several years ago, a friend of many years and literary agent, Calvin Edwards, called me suggesting I meet a couple of girls from Iran. He said he believed their story needed to be put in a book. I responded with high interest and that was the beginning of a book called Captive in Iran.

Narrow Escape

BRENDA JACOBSON

L ondon, with all its history and the winding lanes that weave their way back in time—I love it! So a few years ago when my son decided to go to a short-term Bible school there, I wanted to take him. Like every mom, I was going to miss him and I wanted to picture him in the surroundings he would be in as well as creating lasting memories.

We went to Oxford and then walked around Stonehenge. We took in the British Museum and took a tour of Buckingham Palace. The thing that was on the top of my son's list was spending an afternoon reading in a park in London.

Hyde Park was the chosen destination. We set up a meeting time and we both went our separate directions to enjoy the rare perfect afternoon. I watched him walk away, book under his arm, beginning his adventure away from me.

It was a beautiful day and I wanted to explore the park and spend some time praying for my son as he was venturing out of my "nest." I decided to take a tip from my son and found a peaceful, secluded bench, complete with gently rustling leaves and slight breeze to add to the calm as I lay down and began to pray.

After some time, an unrelated thought pushed its way into my mind. *Open your eyes!* I blinked away the sunshine and noticed a man about seventy-five feet away, walking directly toward me. He was looking down at the red rope he had wound around each hand.

Another thought appeared: *What possible uses could he have for that rope?* I could only come up with one—*strangling.* I calmly looked around and noticed a hedge of bushes a few feet behind the bench I was lying on. The man moved closer as a third thought pushed to the forefront of my mind: *Get up and walk quickly down the hill.* There was no fear or panic, just a simple act of obedience to the promptings. As I got up and started walking down the hill, I glanced over my shoulder at him. My movement had caught him off guard and our eyes met for just a moment. They were chilling—it confirmed his evil intent.

I turned back and kept walking confidently away. After a few minutes I looked over my shoulder again and he was gone. At this point, the reality of what had almost happened became real—and I was finished with my serene adventure in the park and walked back to the hotel to wait for my son.

After dropping my son off at school, I headed over the pond to my home in Oregon, feeling the sadness every mom feels when their child grows up and leaves home. A couple days after arriving home, I got a phone call from my friend, Sheri Rose, who asked, "Brenda, what happened on Wednesday while you were in England?" I said, "What do you mean?" wondering how she had already heard about my trip. She continued, "Last Wednesday, the Lord woke me up to pray for you because you were about to be murdered."

I was stunned. We calculated the time difference between the West Coast and England. It was perfectly clear that the Lord woke Sheri Rose to pray for me at the same time I lay on that bench in Hyde Park with the man approaching who had the rope wrapped around his hands.

A Father's Heart

ALFY FRANKS

In the city of Bombay there are more than three hundred thousand prostitutes. About 60 percent of them have been kidnapped from other places in India or Nepal and literally sold into the flesh trade. Today, young girls between age eleven and thirteen fetch around £2,000 in Bombay. Once these children are sold into brothels, they are confined like prisoners, many of them without clothes so they cannot escape. They are forced to satisfy the list of rich customers who will pay any amount of money for virgins or young girls, in the belief they will renew their youth.

Our teams in Bombay, very much burdened about this situation, asked one of our former Operation Mobilization (OM) girls to work with these women. Naomi was very effective and was able to take many girls back to their homes in the south after they were rescued.

There were two rescue homes Naomi visited constantly. After she led these girls to the Lord Jesus Christ, she found their parents and their families and sent them back home. But although some people believed OM had a huge work among Bombay's prostitutes, we were not really even scratching the surface.

One time a father and his younger son came to us from Kathmandu, Nepal. The man told us that his daughter and another girl, both about fourteen years old, had been taken by an old man in Kathmandu under the pretext that he was going to find jobs for them in India. Of course, the girls were sold into brothels in Bombay. When the man was finally apprehended by the police, he confessed what he had done.

One of the churches in Kathmandu who knew us wrote to the girl's father and assured him that if he went to see the OM India people, they would find his daughter. So with great hope and expectation this father arrived at our office in Bombay.

I felt like the king to whom Naaman appealed for the healing of leprosy. I said in despair, "How in the world can I find your little daughter among three hundred thousand prostitutes? And in a place where their keepers have such a terrible power over them that it is impossible even for police to penetrate their strongholds?"

Anyway, we told the story to Naomi, and she went to see another social worker who is a believer. They went about making inquiries to see what they could do. We were discouraged, but we kept praying that God would have mercy on this father. As a father myself, I knew the agony that he was going through.

It was during the course of one afternoon, when he and a few others were walking up and down the street in a red-light area, praying, that something made him stop and look up. His eyes focused on an upper-story window of a building. And there, beyond all hope or reason, he recognized his own daughter looking down at him. The girl immediately signaled him not to make any disturbance, but to go back and inform the police. Her father found Naomi, and she and the social worker went to the authorities.

By the time the police got to the house, the girl had been tied up and hidden. Finally, however, by God's grace, she was rescued. She later described how desperate she had become. That afternoon she was sleeping on her bed when suddenly she heard a voice tell her distinctly to go and look out the window. She obeyed, and the next moment sighted her father walking down the street. When he stopped and looked up, she was almost overcome.

The father very naturally wanted to take his children home at once, but Naomi restrained him. She convinced him that the gang would see that he didn't even reach the railway station alive. Naomi went back to the police and made certain the man and his children had a police escort all the way home to Kathmandu.

A Hug to End All Hugs

Bob Griffin

It was late 1956, and we were on final approach to land at a tiny airstrip in the jungle of eastern Ecuador. A few minutes earlier the clearing had been swarming with happily waving Jivaro people. Now everyone had disappeared. Something had frightened them. That was bad news.

My passenger, veteran missionary Frank Drown, had asked me several weeks earlier to consider making this special flight. "But," he warned, "pray about it. It might be dangerous." Now I knew why.

We were especially wary because only a few weeks earlier five of our missionary friends had been speared to death just a few miles to the north, by people then known as Auca. The Jivaros to whom we were hoping to pay a visit were just as fierce, with a centuries-old reputation as head-shrinking killers.

Frank knew that. He had been working among some of them for ten years, learning the language, making friends, and developing trust. Now he was asking me to help him with a special project. He wanted to keep alive a peaceful contact his Gospel Missionary Union colleague, Roger Youderian, had initiated with the neighboring hostile group, but was unable to continue. Youderian was one of the five missionaries killed by the Auca savagery.

Frank had told me that my friend, mission pilot Nate Saint, had landed only twice on Youderian's unfinished airstrip. Being asked to complete a difficult landing on a tricky airstrip was enough to give this green, first-term mission pilot ample cause to pray, but that wasn't the half of it. Frank said the people were so mercurial and explosive in their fear of all but intimate tribal members that he could not be sure how we would be received. He thought we would be welcomed even though he hadn't met any of them. He was known to this group only by reputation—but a good one, he thought—as friend to the Jivaros.

Frank didn't know that not long before, angry warriors from this group intent on killing him had lain in ambush alongside a jungle trail. Their chief, Tsantiacu, and his men were in a rage because Frank had helped save the life of one of their worst enemies. To kill was the only response they knew. Later, when recounting the incident, they were still nonplussed that on the day Frank passed by, not one of them, try as he might, could move his trigger finger.

Only days before making this special flight, I had flown overhead to survey the landing area. Sure enough, the strip was a white-knuckle one, but adequate. Best of all, the people had waved a happy welcome. From our perch two hundred feet above, they seemed to be giving every indication of friendliness, welcoming the gifts we dropped.

Now there wasn't anyone to wave. Everyone had disappeared.

By now I was committed to land, so we continued the approach and touched down, still apparently without any welcoming party. Frank jumped out as we rolled to a stop. Grabbing my arm, he ordered, "You stay here, keep the engines running, be ready to leave any second." Then he started walking back down our landing path. He hadn't gone twenty paces when three men silently moved out from the jungle at the far end of the strip. In the middle was Chief Tsantiacu, waving a gun in one hand and with the other motioning us to go away. His warriors, brandishing their guns, added a grim emphasis as they danced threateningly three steps forward, then three back.

"I'm your friend, Panchu," Frank shouted as he advanced. That only seemed to excite them more. My stomach was churning. *I'll have to be the one*, I thought, *to go drag him back when he gets shot.* I was thankful for the idling engine. We could leave in a hurry if we needed to.

But we didn't need to. In a flash the mood changed. The chief, realizing Frank wasn't an enemy, quickly changed his threatening gestures to those of welcome. Frank got a big hug, and they danced around slapping each other on the back. I shut off the engine and joined them for my hug—one I'll never forget.

Suddenly the chief changed his mood again, pushing us off and fixing us with his piercing gaze. "Why did you shoot at us from the plane?" he demanded.

Now we knew. The engine had backfired when I throttled back to land, as it often did. I hadn't thought twice about it, but to them it meant only one thing: We were shooting at them.

We laugh now at their mistake, but it wasn't funny then. That simple misunderstanding of our good intentions could have spoiled the entire day.

Praise God, it didn't. Six weeks later, on a subsequent visit, Chief Tsantiacu turned his life over to the One who, two millennia earlier, had called another persecutor and killer of Christians to repentance. And like that apostle, when the chief turned from being a seeker of heads to a seeker of hearts, he got a hug to end all hugs—from Jesus Himself.

Under Fire

EXCERPTED FROM *THE TOUCH OF THE MASTER*

Operation Mobilization (OM) South Africa sent its first team into Mozambique in 1990, knowing they would be facing tough conditions. Fifteen years of a war that was still going on had demolished the country's agricultural support system. This meant no food, no work, and no money. Medical aid was nonexistent. Children's sores were treated with battery acid; other people walked around with cancer, gangrene, malaria, and bilharzia. The team planned to focus on medical aid and building projects, children's evangelism, and discipleship of believers.

The OM-ers traveled roads that were heavily patrolled by armed soldiers. Vehicles, shot to pieces and burnt out, littered the roadside. Most locals habitually carried weapons and hand grenades.

One night two opposing rebel forces opened fire near where the team had set up camp. We had never lain so close to mother earth or prayed so desperately, realizing that any bullet could mean our final breath. Eight civilians were killed that night, and hundreds of houses burnt, destroying the little that people had left.

The day after the attack, a lady who lived across from us had this story to tell:

> I saw three heavily armed rebel soldiers coming down the road, heading straight for your camp. Just as they were entering the gate they suddenly stopped. Their faces displayed total shock, as if they'd had the fright of their lives. They turned around and ran as quickly as their legs could carry them!

What sight had kept the rebels from their purpose? The team would never know. But they could go on with their work after that, filled with a comforting sense of being surrounded by unseen forces.

Typhoon!

Debbie Meroff

I was just one among a shipload of seasick mariners who thanked God for reaching Japan's shores safely that August of 1996. The *MV Doulos* had cast off from her previous port of Shanghai a day early, after our captain became aware of a dangerously advancing typhoon. The pilot who was to guide us down the Huangpu and Yangtze Rivers told him he was afraid the tide was not full enough. If the *Doulos* had sailed only a half-hour later, he would have been right. Our ship would have been forced to anchor for another twelve hours. And the next day we would have run directly into mega-typhoon Herb.

Even so, our three-hundred-plus staff and crew were warned to expect heavy weather. Vehicles and equipment on deck were securely lashed and personal items were safely stowed. As the 180-mph storm ran in back of the ship toward Taiwan, most of us were remembering the other occasions that summer when God had protected us.

While we were tied up in Subic Bay, Philippines, we were stunned by the news that a typhoon was on its way toward Naha, Japan—exactly where our ship would have been if we had not had an unexpected cancellation. And on the way to Shanghai, the *Doulos* had just managed to run ahead of another violent typhoon called Gloria. Although Herb kicked up sizable seas and few of us cared to swallow anything beyond bread and seasick tablets on the memorable passage to Japan, everyone was aware of how much worse it could have been.

But just as the *Doulos* came into calm seas outside Kagoshima harbor on the morning of August 2, the engine quit. A turbo charger had suddenly malfunctioned. The captain was forced to call tugboats to tow the *Doulos* to her berth.

A few days later on August 5th, Captain Graeme Bird and his staff began tracking another typhoon that seemed to be heading in our direction. Typhoon Kirk's behavior was worrying, revealing itself to be both erratic and powerful. In the next few days the storm succeeded in putting one vessel aground and sinking another, its twenty-two passengers forced to abandon ship.

On Monday the 12th of August, there was no longer any doubt the typhoon was headed directly for Kagoshima. The port authority ordered all vessels to clear the harbor. Ships that could make a run for it or ride at anchor normally had a good chance of escaping major damage. But the *Doulos* had no options. The replacement parts of our engine hadn't arrived yet. We could only brace ourselves and pray for the best.

Deck and engine crewmen, forewarned, had already been working hard, laying on extra mooring lines and lashing down every movable object fore and aft with steel wires. Nothing, however, had prepared me for the horror of suddenly being jerked out of my sleep at about 3:00 a.m. on August 13th, when the full fury of Typhoon Kirk slammed into the *Doulos*. Fighting the ship's violent list to starboard I staggered to my feet and dressed quickly. Then I headed toward my office, anxious to check the safety of my computer. On the way I ran into a dozen deckmen in orange slickers. The expression on their faces didn't reassure me.

Once back in my cabin, I lay down on my bunk, fully dressed, reliving a rush of memories that threatened to swamp me with fear. I had been aboard the old *Logos* back in 1988 when she was shipwrecked off South America. Though it was long ago, I could still remember every detail of that January night—the shock, the fear, and the enormous sense of loss.

A few years later I had sailed to South America again with the *Logos II*. In one port we were hit by a disastrous storm, and although we had come out of it without major damage, we had seen ships sunk all around us. People had lost their lives. I was aware now of what could happen in violent storms, even to ships as large as the *Doulos*, when they were tied up and helpless.

At around 4:00 a.m., I heard someone knocking on the cabin doors in my section. I recognized First Officer Steve Wallace's voice, advising cabin occupants to get up and dressed. Families, he added quietly, might want to prepare an emergency kit—just in case it should become necessary to evacuate the ship.

That did it. I had a horrifying sense of déjà vu, as though the nightmares of the past had all come upon me once again. Panic seized me. I flung open my cabin door and Steve Wallace saw my face.

"We're alright, Debbie! Nothing is going to happen to us."

"That's what they said before!" I wailed. I couldn't seem to control my voice or the tears that slipped down my face. "It's just like what happened before! We could sink right where we are."

"We won't! Listen to me. I know this ship. I've checked everything out. Trust me, OK?"

I respected Steve's long sea experience. I knew I could trust his assessment. I nodded, unable to speak.

While waiting for the winds to spend themselves, I drew comfort from the Psalms. My *Daily Bread* devotional thought for that day also held a particularly relevant assurance: "God does not keep us from life's storms; He walks with us through them." I was learning something through Typhoon Kirk.

When Captain Bird called the crew together later that day, he confided that his greatest fear had been that one of the several large barges anchored near us might break loose and drive into our hull. This would have meant immediate evacuation at the worst of the storm.

Winds reached up to 220 kph or *Stormforce 13 or 14*—"off the scale." But fortunately for the *Doulos*, the edge of the typhoon's eye did not hit broadside but astern on the port side, pushing the ship against the quay. Gusts caused a sharp list to starboard from ten degrees all the way to fifteen. Unsecured articles went flying. Rain and seawater was driven through doors and porthole hatches, flooding starboard decks and cabins. Overflowing sewage lines also backed into some of the accommodation areas. Damages to books and equipment amounted to approximately $7,000.

"But we had the right berth," asserted the captain. "The wind came astern, and at any other berth we would have been blown off, losing the mooring lines. We did worry about lines washing off from the high waves. That would have been a problem. We were also concerned about the fender (protecting the hull from damage against the quayside). But it lasted through the storm, and only broke off at the end. By God's providence it was there as long as we needed it!"

The captain also made us dramatically aware of God's intervention in another way. He stated, "If we had gotten the engine part we needed, we would have had to sail. We couldn't have anchored—our anchor cable isn't long enough for the deep water here. So we just had to make all the preparations we could, and they had to work!"

Of course, some would simply call it a piece of luck that the *Doulos* managed to evade at least three typhoons and that our engine gave out only when we reached the harbor outside

Kagoshima. They would also claim it was coincidence that a missing turbo charger had kept us in port during Typhoon Kirk, when three large ships that did go to anchor went aground. But don't try to convince any of us who were aboard God's ship that summer of 1996. We know better!

Arrested in the Ivory Coast

John Van Diest

Nigeria is far from being a Christian nation, but groups like TEAM (The Evangelical Alliance Mission), now ECWA (Evangelical Churches of West Africa), have faithfully presented the claims of Christ during the past century. And this has resulted in a growing church and missionary outreach.

During the late 1980s several leaders from the U.S. Christian booksellers industry were invited to evaluate the Christian bookstores in Nigeria and recommend how to strengthen them. I was privileged to be a part of that.

We met in Brussels, flew south through Monrovia and Ivory Coast on our way to Lagos, Nigeria. En route the pilot announced we needed to stop in Abidjan, Ivory Coast, for fuel.

Upon arrival at the airport in Abidjan, we were told we were under arrest! We were simply told that we needed visas to land in Ivory Coast. We were taken to a facility, a whitewashed room with dark and dirty marks at the buttock and head level. We were not concerned until we were told our case would be dealt with in the morning. Since it was around midnight we realized it might be a long night with a guard positioned at the entrance.

Soon the door opened and the man identified himself as

from the UN and offered to help. He mentioned that he was an American and served in the Congo. I asked him if he had ever met my missionary uncle, Dr. Leslie Chaffee. "Oh," he said, "we are friends!" The man (maybe he was an angel!) offered to talk to the authorities about our plight. He informed the police chief, and after an apology, each of us was given a "fancy hut on stilts" right on the waterfront plus a wonderful breakfast of bacon and eggs the next morning.

As most of you know, foreign travel is usually full of surprises, particularly in developing countries. We knew we were in God's hands and the evidence of His protection was a cause for praise.

I'm still curious whether the man who helped rescue us was a UN agent or a heavenly agent.

Walking Through the Night

CAREY HAURI

I stepped off the bus and began to trudge up the hill, pulling my coat tighter about me to keep out the chilly Hungarian night air. My steps were laborious; every movement was restricted by the chiropractic back brace strapped around my torso. I hated wearing it but knew that I should obey doctor's orders.

I could hear someone walking behind me. *Probably just someone else on his way home,* I thought. I finally got to the top of the stairway and started walking along the main street, which led the rest of the way up the hill. I could still hear the footsteps behind me. They were speeding up and getting closer, which didn't surprise me. My back brace really slowed me down.

Then, suddenly, someone grabbed me from behind. An arm gripped me tightly around my neck. I struggled to free myself but couldn't. I craned my head around to try and catch a glimpse of my attacker. It was dark so I couldn't see much except the shadowy outline of a man, shorter than I but stronger, with dark hair. The man mumbled a few words in Hungarian, which I couldn't understand. I didn't know what to do. *This is it,* I thought, *my life is over.*

I screamed and screamed, hoping that maybe someone

would hear me and come to help. I couldn't think of anything else to say or do. My mind was so numb that I couldn't even think to pray and cry out to God. The limited Hungarian I knew completely deserted me. I was totally incapable of coherent thought. I grabbed the arm that was around my neck and tried to pry it loose, but the man continued to grip me tightly. My legs buckled and I found myself kneeling on the road. With my raised right arm I instinctively shielded my face. I felt something press hard into my back.

At that moment my brain started working again. *I think I'm being stabbed*, I thought to myself, surprised by such remarkable objectivity and logic. I waited for the pain but, strangely enough, didn't feel any. All I could feel was something digging into my back. I continued to scream as I knelt helplessly in the dirt. Then, unexpectedly, my attacker loosened his grip, and I heard the sound of running feet. I turned around in time to see his shadowy figure race off down a dark, narrow lane leading back down the hill.

I staggered to my feet. My hand felt wet. I stared at it, dripping with blood. I started to cry. My other hand was fine so I used it to hold my back in a vain attempt to stop the blood that I expected was flowing from there also. Slowly, I walked up the hill, sobbing uncontrollably. If I could just make it home!

It was at that moment that I awoke. *"Thank God!"* I breathed in relief. It was only a bad dream.

I tried to turn over and go back to sleep but a sharp pain jolted me wide awake. Something was digging into my back. Gingerly I reached behind me and my fingers found a plastic tube dangling over the side of the bed.

What's that doing there? I wondered groggily. Then it hit me: I hadn't been dreaming at all. I looked around the room—a hospital ward. How had I gotten there? Then I remembered.

I had only gone a few steps up the hill when a young couple

had come running toward me. They must have heard my screams. They asked if I was okay and gently helped me walk to a small bar halfway up the hill. I'd passed the place many times but had never ventured inside.

As we entered, people immediately flocked around me, clucking with concern. The barmaid took a cloth and wrapped it around my bleeding hand. It stung but looked worse than it actually was. I pointed at my back but no one could see anything wrong with it.

I removed my jacket. Everyone gasped when they saw the huge patch of blood that had seeped through the several layers of clothing I was wearing. Someone rang the police and the ambulance. Several men raced from the bar to find my attacker, but I was sure they'd never catch him. It was too easy to disappear in the tangle of streets and lanes that crisscrossed the hill. By the time the ambulance arrived I'd calmed down enough to realize that I wasn't going to die just yet, after all.

It was a bumpy ride to the hospital. I gripped the metal rail bordering the stretcher with my fingers and toes so that I wouldn't slide around too much or bounce off the mattress altogether. After arrival I was wheeled around on a stretcher and examined by a number of doctors, including a neurosurgeon who spoke excellent English. They all shook their heads in disbelief when they heard what had happened and promptly blamed the new Western influences flooding the country.

Someone stitched and dressed the stab wound in my back: a horizontal gash three centimeters long and two centimeters deep. A tube was inserted to drain the blood from the wound.

"You're lucky," the neurosurgeon said. "A few millimeters either way and the knife could have hit your spinal cord or punctured your lung."

"I'm not 'lucky,'" I told him, "God was looking after me!"

The doctor thought for a moment. "That doesn't make sense.

If God was looking after you, why did He let this happen to you in the first place? He wasn't looking after you very well, was He?"

I thought about that and remembered my back brace. What would have happened if I hadn't been wearing it? The knife had actually glanced off the top edge of the brace so wearing it had spared me the full force of the blow. My hated brace had actually acted as a life-saving shield.

"Yes," I finally answered the doctor. "God was definitely looking after me. I don't understand why this has happened, but it could have been a lot worse."

As I lay there the conversation came back to me. *I don't understand, Lord*, I thought. *You saved my life by making sure I was wearing my back brace when I was attacked, but why did You even let it happen at all? Why did You let that man attack me? Do You really care about me?*

My faith in the Lord was strong enough to ask questions and not be afraid of the answers. I tried to sleep, but the questions continued to echo inside my head, demanding answers that didn't come. I felt very alone.

Gradually I saw that I had a choice to make. I could blame God for allowing the incident to happen—didn't I have a right to be angry with Him? At the same time, I also realized that if I took that road, I could end up becoming a very bitter and disillusioned person, my relationship with the Lord being reduced to tatters.

My other option was to simply accept what had happened and trust that God had allowed it for reasons that maybe I would never understand. My faith would be severely tested, but if it was as real and solid as I believed it to be, shouldn't it also be strong enough to get me through this? What good is faith if it can't carry me through the tough times? It's one thing to trust in God when life is good, but doesn't the true test of faith come through the hard times?

I knew that for me there was only one way to go. I'd been in difficult situations before, and God had never let me down. How could I turn away from Him now? If anything, I needed God in a special way now more than ever. The thought of getting through this terrible ordeal on my own, without Him, was a worse nightmare than the one I had just experienced.

"Okay, God, I don't understand why this has happened, but I'm going to keep believing in You anyway and trust that You will somehow use this for good," I prayed at some time in the early hours of the morning. *"Help me to learn whatever it is that You want to teach me through this."*

A deep peace came over me, and I sensed the presence of Jesus in a way I had never experienced before. It was as if He was sitting on the bed beside me. I fell asleep, secure in the knowledge that I really wasn't alone.

Two weeks later I was back at work. Although it took a while for me to recover completely, I surprised others and myself at how I came through the experience relatively unscathed. Despite a physical scar to remind me that the attack had actually happened, the incident didn't seem to leave any long-term psychological scars.

For a while I was afraid to go out at night on my own, and at first, even during the day I would become uneasy when people walked behind me. As the weeks and months passed, those fears slowly dissipated. In the hospital I had read Roman 8:35-39 a lot and those precious verses were my strength. *Nothing* could separate me from the love of Christ! Paul even mentioned a "sword." As far as I was concerned a knife was close enough. I was comforted by the fact that God had my situation covered!

Today I still don't understand why God allowed this attack, and I possibly never will. But that's no longer the main issue for me. What's important to me is that my faith was tested, and it withstood the test. God didn't let me down.

What Happened on March 9?

DAVID JEREMIAH (REWRITTEN BY JOHN VAN DIEST)

During World War II the Thirty-Fifth Infantry Division was advancing east in the Rhineland region of West Germany. The area was wooded, and many soldiers had been badly injured by German fire.

American soldier Spencer Jumeary was part of an assigned group to replace the previous company of Allied wounded soldiers. The scene was messy, and it appeared that the Americans were greatly outnumbered by the Nazis. Spencer and his fellow soldiers were ordered to advance, making them very vulnerable. They prayed and ran for their lives. Instantly, out of nowhere, a cloud obscured the line of fire of the Germans. The Americans found safety in the deep woods opposite the enemy lines.

"This has to be God!" Spencer concluded and waited to see what would happen next. Immediately after all the Americans had arrived in the safety of the woods, the cloud vanished.

The Nazis, still thinking that the Americans were on the other side of the field, radioed the position to their artillery. Minutes later the vacated position was bombed to bits.

Sometime later, after Spencer had arrived back home to Dallas, Texas, his mother asked, "Son, what happened on the morning of March 9? A lady at church called me that morning and said the Lord awakened her at one o'clock and impressed upon her that you were in danger. She said she interceded in prayer for several hours. She said the last thing she prayed was, 'Lord, whatever danger Spencer is in, just cover him with a cloud.'"

Prisoners, and Yet...

David Bradley

T he interrogator sitting at the scarred wooden desk stroked the corners of his mustache like the archetypal villain of a melodrama. He tried again, unconvincingly, to allay our fears. "Don't worry. Everything will be okay. Just sign these statements and I'll let you go."

Merv and I were just far enough away that he couldn't hear our muttered exchange. "I don't trust this guy any further than I can spit," I said. "He already told us not to worry several times. If there's nothing to worry about, then why are we still here after five hours of questioning?"

My Canadian companion and I had finished four weeks of backpacking in the Himalayan Mountains of Nepal that autumn of 1988. I was a seasoned trekker, but on that thirty-first day when the Phidim police took us into custody and thoroughly searched our belongings, I had to wonder if it was the end of the trail for me.

The dark, arrogant eyes of the District Superintendent of Police narrowed. "You came here breaking the law with your propaganda. Why? Why did you come to Phidim? Answer all the questions and you will be free to go home. Tell me. Where did you get these books?"

His air of self-importance was raising my hackles. "We've told you before. There is nothing illegal in our possession." Did he see through my bluff? I didn't need a stethoscope to hear my heart pounding a staccato beat on my eardrums. "You have held us against our will despite the fact that you've caught us doing nothing wrong. We only came to this town because it's the first place we could get a bus back to Kathmandu."

"Besides," interjected Merv, "you found our permits and passports in order. You've refused to let us talk to a lawyer, which is a violation of international law."

The DSP was finding it hard to follow our English. He turned to his translator and began gesturing toward our baggage. It didn't make any sense. Our porter's sack and rucksack had already been searched once. What were they looking for?

"Open the bags," he ordered one of his men. "Empty them. I want to see everything."

Sleeping bags, ponchos, two packets of granola, a large cooking pot and ladle, and several empty burlap sacks were soon strewn about the floor. The sacks had been full to the brim only a few days before. My qualms eased slightly, knowing that Christian books identical to those found in our shoulder bags during the first search would never be found.

"What's this?" The police chief, second-in-command, grabbed a couple of innocuous-looking cardboard squares and tore them apart, exposing two small records in paper sleeves. A knowing grin crept from ear to ear. My stomach knotted.

"Where is the gramophone?"

"What gramophone?"

"Where is the gramophone?" The chief's fat hands tore at the side pockets of our rucksack and brought more records into view. His grin widened. He continued searching: toothbrush, pocketknife, clothes, and a handful of loose papers.

I groaned inwardly and rolled my eyes in self-disgust. *Oh, no. Lord, don't let him see what's in those papers.* Merv looked at me questioningly. *It's my journal. It tells everything about the trek—where we've been, who we met, how much literature was distributed. Everything.*

Both of us stared at the papers, but they refused to disappear. "What is it?" demanded the superintendent in Nepali. The other officer shrugged. "It's written in English…" Delighted discovery suddenly stabbed the thick air. "It's a diary!" The translator read a few lines to them, and the two officers turned their gaze upon us. Neither one was smiling now.

Merv and I and three of our porters were placed in a custody cell ten feet wide and ten feet long. It was the first day of what was to stretch into many long months of uncertainty.

After four days, everyone agreed the porters were not guilty of anything and they were finally released. We gave them money, a sleeping bag, and a cooking pot. Inside the sleeping bag was a note intended for Connie, my wife, telling her we needed a lawyer.

At our first court appearance that day the judge had indicated we could be liable for three years in prison. Six years was the sentence for successfully proselytizing (indicated by a convert's baptism). Three years was the standard sentence for anyone "attempting to proselytize," which could even mean preaching; and three years for "disturbing the Hindu community." Later the judge changed his estimate to between three and six years. I knew he had already made up his mind that we were guilty.

Day eight: Merv and I were transferred to the main part of the prison. We found our own places on the floor and quickly made friends with five other men who gathered around and tried to teach us some Nepali. I made mistakes so they wouldn't realize that I knew the language. When I asked the friendliest of them why he was in prison he thumped his chest and declared, "I die a man"—meaning he had killed a man. Later we discovered that sixteen of our fellow inmates were charged with murder and eight with theft.

We also began to learn about some of the punishments imposed upon these prisoners during police custody, before reaching prison. Leg irons or manacles attached to the wall were common. Many endured torture, strung up by the feet and beaten with rods on their feet and bodies. The police even stuck pins under their nails and shoved chili up their noses. I was filled with outrage at such injustices and at my inability to do anything about them.

We were allowed to roam the compound inside the high walls during the day. Near the end of the second week, while I was doing exercises, my foot slipped into a hole. The other inmates massaged it with hot oil but my ankle continued to give me pain. Only months later, after my release, did an X-ray show the ankle bone had been fractured.

Bedbugs and minor colds also kept us awake many nights. The worst of our plight, however, was not knowing what was going on outside. We had been refused bail, and although we had sent a message to our embassies via the police in Kathmandu, we had no idea if it was delivered. It hurt to think of Connie and my son Jason—only five months old when I last saw him—trying to carry on without me. And how were my parents back in the States dealing with this? I told myself that God knew how to care for my family better than I did.

Four weeks of imprisonment passed and we were shown court documents with fabricated statements by "witnesses," all saying we had sold books, records and tapes, and even preached. Strangely, all appeared to know my name as well. I was sure these people had been forced into writing what they did under fear of police retaliation.

Day fifty: A friend arrived! South Asia Area Coordinator Mike Wakely had traveled all the way from England to the isolated mountains of Nepal to bring us news, food, and mail.

Among the letters was a picture of Connie and Jason. It was a weird feeling not to recognize my son. He had changed so much in the almost three months since I'd seen him! Merv and I were tremendously encouraged by the messages from family and friends. Oh, the joy of being loved!

Three days later we received a surprise visit from the consul of the U.S. Embassy. He told us the State Department had registered a complaint with the Nepal government for not notifying the embassy of their detention of an American citizen. The consul said he hadn't known of our existence until a few days before, when Mike and two other friends visited him.

Day seventy-three: We heard on the radio that drug barons had kidnapped two missionaries in Colombia. How insignificant our plight seemed in comparison to theirs! Those men stood a good chance of not coming out of their ordeal alive. In our confinement, Merv and I were able even to send and receive mail. We began to pray for those two missionaries. Psalm 69:33 would always hold new meaning for me: "He does not despise his imprisoned people."

Day seventy-nine: The dread of being separated for a long time from Connie and Jason was growing larger. I had begun to feel that I HAD to be released. Connie's letters reflected her struggles. Jason had been sick. My concern for them was overwhelming. Could I surrender it to God? It hurt, it hurt! I wanted to be reunited with them. But I didn't want to sell out either. That night Merv and I sang songs of praise. My heart was heavy, and I needed to lift it up to the Lord.

On January 18, day eighty-four, we had more visitors. My first anxious question was about Jason's condition. He was fine, these friends assured me. And it appeared that the news about our situation was spreading. The story had been aired on Canadian television and hit major newspapers coast to coast; my mother had been on TV in the States, and all Christian publications carried the report. Our visitors brought us a Walkman and tapes, and even smuggled in some books in Nepali that were well received by the other inmates.

Our prison cell was getting crowded. In three months the population had grown from twenty-eight to forty-three. The judge called us in again and told us he didn't like Christians and wanted to see all Christian organizations out of Nepal. Not encouraging.

Day ninety-one: At last I was able to see Connie and Jason again, face-to-face! We held each other for a long time. Connie was definitely thinner in the face, but she looked good. Poor Jason was tired from the long trip. We were allowed only two hours together, but they planned to stay for eight or ten days and we were able to spend much of it together.

On January 26 we were back in court, this time for the cross-examination of witnesses. The Nepali lawyer we'd obtained seemed confident of our acquittal, but he still hadn't gotten a copy of my journal and thus didn't know all I'd written! The grim news was that we were up for six-year sentences, not three. Only four out of the eleven witnesses appeared, and their statements were not consistent. One man even admitted that he had signed his name to the prepared statement only because the police told him to. That took courage. I prayed that God would bless him for it.

Saying goodbye to Connie and Jason was hard, although our week together did a lot to settle my fears for them. Connie was planning to return for our final hearing, set for February 28. I sensed she was pessimistic about our release. Merv also had periods of depression. The district officer told us that the judge could make a decision on our case at the hearing. He asked if we would prefer to transfer to Kathmandu if we were convicted—a disconcerting question.

It was difficult to know how much was being done about our situation in official circles. We were now getting letters of support from twenty-five to thirty countries around the world and guessed there were thousands praying for us. This action was a result of the Christian network.

The Canadian First Secretary came to visit on February 5th, the same day Merv suddenly got very sick. He had a terrible time breathing, and the doctor had to be called. He thought it was bronchial asthma. The next day Merv was unable to eat. Proper health care was very far away, but we prayed, and quite soon, thankfully, his condition began to improve.

The week before our hearing we received a lot of encouragement from the other prisoners. Ser, who had been a friend from the start and would be spending the next ten years in jail, declared outright that he was a Christian now and nothing could make him change. I challenged another man, Mohan, who said he was going to follow the Lord when he got out. A big surprise came when someone from outside the prison came and asked me for a Christian book. I sensed that God was bringing things to a head. Merv and I also believed that God had done something good inside us through these months of imprisonment.

On the afternoon of February 27, our friend Mike, the U.S. Embassy Consul, and an assistant, the Canadian Consular Officer, plus an American reporter arrived in Phidim. Connie couldn't come, but she had written. She said she feared that we would not get released, and Merv's mother felt the same. That hit us hard. From other letters we knew that this was a day of fasting and prayer throughout the OM world. In the evening Merv and I committed ourselves to God and had what we hoped would be our last communion service in prison. Since we had no bread or crackers, we substituted chocolate!

On February 28 Merv and I packed up all of our belongings in case we were set free. The time passed slowly until 10 a.m. when we were finally called to go to court. The judge asked to see us in his office.

"What do you want today?" he asked. Merv replied, "We want what God wants." The judge didn't like that answer. I spoke up and said we wanted to be found not guilty, and he dismissed us.

Our lawyer had convinced the judge to allow the curious local people outside to hang in the windows and crowd into the courtroom. After the judge convened the trial, the court lawyer gave a spirited, five-minute argument on why we should be given a six-year sentence. Our Nepali lawyer then spoke for over an hour, explaining why we should be set free.

His appearance and presentation were impressive. At one point this unsaved man took a school textbook of world religions and read several pages about Jesus! Quite a few nodded their heads in agreement when the lawyer pointed out that this was a government-sanctioned book, and if we were sentenced for our books then so must every teacher in Nepal! The judge agreed with this argument. We were given a two-hour recess, and then he returned with the verdict: not guilty! MERV AND I WERE ACQUITTED!

The legal proceedings were completed and we returned to the prison, only to find our belongings had already been placed outside. We were not allowed inside to say good-bye to anyone, which made us sad. We stood at the small door and spoke to Ser and the rest of our friends as well as we could.

Disturbed by rumors that Merv and I would be taken into Kathmandu under police escort, our friends urged us to hurry out of Phidim. We carried our bags to a jeep parked on a hill overlooking the prison. When that was done I shouted down to the inmates, "JESUKO JAI!"—"Victory to Jesus!" They responded, "JAI!"—"Praise to the Lord!"

We piled into the jeeps. Twisting and turning up the mountain we could look far below to the prison from which Merv and I had so often looked up, tracing the route to freedom. Now, at last, we were on that road. Nepal would never again be the same for us. And we ourselves would never be the same.

Miracles of Provision

This same God who takes care of me
will supply all your needs from his glorious riches,
which have been given to us in Christ Jesus.

Philippians 4:19

Miracles of Provision

"Angels are only servants—spirits sent to care for people who will inherit salvation" (Hebrews 1:14). The stories of divine provision abound. The main job description for angels is to serve, protect, guide, encourage, and deliver us.

The needs of people may not be as critical in the West as in other parts of the world. No wonder, then, that many miracle accounts of supernatural provision occur in other lands. However, God's provisional methods are not limited to material things. Comfort, peace, safety, joy, and hope are just a few of the "fruit" God provides for His own.

Fresh Water

BARRY ARNOLD

While piloting a small plane to a remote area of Alaska, I was forced to make an emergency landing. I was flying with my friend Randy Alcorn, my daughter Andrea, and Randy's daughter, Karina. The girls were both age ten at the time. I have told the story to many over the years, and Randy turned on his video camera to document the whole experience.

The four of us were in the airplane when we lost the engine in the mountains. The prop stopped at the ten o'clock position. The altimeter showed fifteen hundred feet above sea level. The fact that God provided a sandbar at just the right moment that we needed a landing strip and we made it down uninjured was truly His grace, but there's another story of God's provision that I've rarely told.

It was a hot day for Alaska—about seventy degrees (in the video Randy is shirtless on the sandbar where we landed), and we didn't have any water to drink. The girls were getting really thirsty. There was a glacial river nearby, but it was so thick with silt that it was almost flowing mud.

We began scouting around, looking for fresh water. We'd been on the ground for about three hours when the girls came running over to where we had set up camp, and they were squealing.

"We found water! There's good water coming out of the ground right by the airplane."

We went over there and sure enough, right by the airplane, where it had been bone-dry gravel three hours before, the clearest, freshest water you ever saw was bubbling up out of the ground. There was all we could drink and then some.

I think of that spring the Lord implanted in that bone-dry gravel bar when I read, "Your love will overflow more and more" (Philippians 1:9). Our lives should be like refreshing spring water to thirsty people.

And by the way, when the helicopter came to rescue us several hours later, the spring that we had drunk from was as muddy as the glacial river.

Fishing in China

CARL LAWRENCE

A man sent to prison for his religious beliefs had four children ages four, eight, ten, and twelve. His wife was made to walk the street with a dunce cap, and the children were treated badly because their father was a "bad" element. The problem was they had no livelihood, and therefore, no food.

In the back of their little house was a small pond. No one had fished there before, but the children made a net and started fishing. They caught enough fish to feed the family. The supply began to multiply. As time went on, they got enough fish not only for their own needs, but to trade for other necessities of life.

Thirteen years later, the father returned from prison. There were no fish in the little pond from that day on; they were no longer needed.

The Bill Has Been Paid

HELEN ROSEVEARE

My cook, Aunzio, and I erected a small, one-room mud-and-thatch building to serve as a clinic for the leprosy patients in Zaire. We sent off to Stanleyville (Kisangani today), 350 miles to the southwest, for the needed medicines, bandages, and equipment.

Eventually the box of supplies arrived. Together, Aunzio and I opened it. He excitedly drew out the large bottle of 10,000 tablets of the new drug Dapsone that had just replaced the painful injections of chaulmoogra oil in the treatment of leprosy. I picked up the bill—4,320 Belgian Congo francs (in 1954, worth 30 British pounds, or about 90.50 in U.S. dollars). Somewhat caustically, perhaps, I reminded God that I had not 50 pence available for paying the bill, let alone 30 pounds. And as He, Almighty God, had led me to start this particular clinic for the treatment of leprosy patients, I was sure that He would pay the bill, which I slipped into my Bible.

The end of the month came. Mission rules demanded that all bills be paid by the end of the month; no debts were allowed. There was no money available to meet this bill of 30 pounds, 50 pence...none. There were no funds from which I could borrow.

I felt concerned. Why had God not provided? Such a sum would be nothing for Him. It was the price of a cow, perhaps, but it was a fortune to me—three or four months' allowance in those days. I went to work on that Saturday morning, the first of the new month, with a sense of grievance against God.

As I returned home at lunchtime, Aunzio encouraged me to hurry, saying there was a brown envelope waiting for me. Another missionary had sent it across, apologizing that he had received it in his mail the previous day and had not noticed that it was addressed to me—from our field leader's office. Aunzio and I opened it together. I shook out the money, which he carefully piled and laboriously counted. I pulled out the statement. The total, in the bottom right-hand corner, came to 4,800 Belgian Congo francs. A quick mental calculation showed the tithe at 480 francs, leaving exactly 4,320 francs.

This total was made up of three gifts, from an unknown couple in North America, from two prayer partners in North Ireland, and from a Girls Crusaders' Union class in southeast England. The North American gift had been on the way for four months, transferred from our Philadelphia office to the London office, from London to Brussels, Brussels to Leopoldville (Isiro). Every transfer involved a certain percentage cost. At the end, the three gifts had arrived together to make the exact sum needed and were designated "for your leprosy work." I did not have a leprosy work when the money was actually given!

The Well and the Wood

ANONYMOUS

It was famine in Central India. For three long years there had been almost no rain at all. The parched earth baked in the furnace sun until great cracks appeared in its surface, cracks so deep that stones dropped therein never touched bottom at all, if one might judge from the lack of sound. There was no food and no water, and little children were dying in the streets everywhere.

The two lady missionaries who stood at the head of things made themselves responsible for the lives of five hundred people. Wheat could be brought into the country from lands far way, and it was brought. So there was food, but the water was giving out.

All over the city, wells were drying up one by one—poor wells, caste wells, and at last even their own well. The need was bitter and desperate. All around lay little children moaning for "Water! Water!" And even grown-ups jostled one another in an agony of mad thirst for the remaining precious drops.

The two lone women walked the compound praying and groaning in spirit. Rising to a white heat of intensity, their supplication burned its way upward into the ear of Him who has, since the world began, heard every such cry of His own.

At length one of them received a promise, and such a peculiar promise—one that seemed not at all applicable. "Every place that the sole of your foot will tread upon I have given you" (Joshua 1:3 NKJV). And on that sure word both despairing feet were firmly planted. "Yea, Lord," she repeated over and over again. "I believe that on this piece of ground, where I now stand, a well shall be given us of Thee."

Gathering together a few men who still had strength to work, she told them of her prayer and its answer. "So now you may begin right here and dig," she commanded. But they only laughed at her.

"Auntie," they said, "we have heard that faraway America is a land of water, even much water, but not so in India. We understand India, and there is no water in this place. There *never* will be water here."

"Dig," was the only reply. And they dug—that is, they began.

Two feet down solid rock was encountered. But some miles away lived a brother missionary, and to him they sent at once an explanation of their difficulty. He came with dynamite and a fuse. A bit of blasting and the rock was conquered. Still, the men laughed derisively in their unbelief. But the faith of the two missionaries never wavered. "Dig," would come the command. And they dug.

Another day went by. Fifteen feet down and no water. Twenty feet down and still no water, not even dampness. Thirty feet down, and suddenly—often God does things suddenly—three streams of crystal water spouted up from the dark bottom of the well. Dropping their tools, the men climbed for their lives up out of that tremendous inflow.

In a very short time the well was full, and all of the five hundred people had enough to spare. Wonder starred their eyes, and gratitude made their hearts tender as they drank, and drank, and drank again. "It is the water of the living God," they said. And never from that day has it failed or ceased to flow. One of the lady missionaries happened to be standing at the edge of the well at the time of the first spouting, and she said it seemed as if an invisible Hand had piped that water from the bowels of the earth, for the three streams shot up vertically from the solid rock.

Outside the compound and some distance away, a company of Englishmen were laboring to establish a cotton gin. They needed water also, and the best of modern well-drilling machinery had been sent out to them from England. Three hundred feet down they bored, straight into the rock, but not a drop of the precious liquid rewarded their efforts. Then they came to the missionaries and said, "Let us put an electric water-finder over your well and learn in what direction the vein runs."

Permission was given, and the buzzing Victrola-like apparatus was set up over the well. But the dial certainly never behaved so erratically before. Round and round it spun, this way and that, and registered—nothing. The Englishmen were astonished. "Why," one of them exclaimed, "there must be no vein of water here at all!" Then, turning to the missionaries, "Your water," he said, "comes straight up from the bowels of the earth, a phenomenon that is quite beyond our understanding."

A wiser Indian standing by ventured in reply, "Ah, Sahib, did you not know? It is the well of the living God!" And the name stands today. All over the countryside people still speak with awe and amazement of the water of the living God.

Again it was famine time. Water was now there in abundance, and wheat to be ground into flour. But there was no wood for the fire to cook it. One cannot live on raw flour. Moreover, there was no money, not even one rupee in the little tin box labeled "general expense." It was time for prayer—asking and faith-talking. And the promise that came now was the familiar

Philippians 4:19, never worn out and available for use as ever. The angel who brought it laid special emphasis on the "shall supply." Together, the two ladies continued in prayer.

A day or two later a man ambled in the front gate and presented himself at the door. "I have wood to sell," he said, "forty carts of it. My home is far away among the hills, so I must sell and start back today. Do the memsahibs wish to take it?"

Did they? Those forty carts would suffice for all their need. They would save lives on the compound, perhaps their own lives. But there was no money to pay. Still, "My God shall supply!"

"Yes," they agreed, "we will take it. Bring in the carts and empty them at the rear of the house."

So the procession began. One cart around, wood weighed and dumped. Two carts, three carts. The ladies watched from the door, then went again to look at the tin box. It was still empty. But "My God shall supply." No use to look for foreign mail with its rare and precious money gifts, for there had been no boat in from America for some days. Still the promise was there.

Back to the front door...seventeen, eighteen, nineteen carts. The man had stated clearly his price for the wood, and it was a fair one, but it might have been ten times as much so far as paying him was concerned. Or would God presently shower rupees out of His heaven? Or perhaps they would be found in His earth! Twenty-seven, twenty-eight carts. "My God shall supply."

Was there a moneyed friend among the Indian Christians? Not one. Would there be a missionary friend with aught to spare? Impossible. Such friends were far away, and even had they been present they would have had nothing to give in famine time. Thirty-eight, thirty-nine carts. And the little tin box so empty!

The fortieth cart swam through a mist of tears as the bullock drew slowly around to the rear. It passed the long veranda, passed also the little Indian postman who was entering with a letter. Strangely enough—and yet not strange at all—it was a registered letter. With a heart that fluttered and skipped a few beats, the missionary took it and quickly broke the seal. The money order within was unfolded, and He had supplied! The sum named was exactly that asked for the wood, not one rupee more, not one less. In a twinkling she had signed it, then turned and paid for the wood.

A few weeks before, news of the great famine had filtered through to far corners of the earth, and hearts were being stirred to pray, even in Central Africa. As they prayed they began to feel a burning urge to give. But giving with them spelled sacrifice also, real, unromantic giving up of rice and calico apparel. Never mind, they would do it anyway, and with joy!

The missionary sold the things brought to him for this purpose, and quite a little sum was gathered. Slowly the letter started, through the jungle down the mighty Congo, and on to the sea, around the Cape of Storms, up the Indian Ocean, into a Bombay bank where it was exchanged; then on to Central India. And it arrived, as you see, on the very day, at the very moment it was needed.

"My God shall supply all your need."

More Company for Dinner!

W. Phillip Keller

The missionary wholeheartedly threw himself into the work that bore the name "Soldiers', Sailors', and Airmen's Christian Association." In British Columbia alone, this organization set up ten main bases to meet the spiritual needs as well as social wants of servicemen.

Amongst all the depots so established, perhaps none came to be more widely known or better loved by the boys and girls in uniform than the missionary's big rambling house in Victoria. For some who trod across its threshold for the first time, perhaps in company with a companion who was a Christian, this became a trysting place with God, for there they had the claims of Christ upon their lives presented to them boldly.

God saw all this and smiled. Much more, though, God Himself was in the work, and under the guidance of His Spirit young men and women from all across Canada came to know Christ in this house as they had never known Him before.

At last the war-weary years dragged their heavy-booted feet away to be forgotten. Civilian life was settling gently and silently back over the scene. It was the end of 1945, and the final details of winding up the work in the big house on Belmont Avenue in Victoria were almost completed. As though it were to be a final farewell, twenty-five servicemen and women had been invited for a New Year's dinner.

It was New Year's Eve, and the missionary and his wife were in the huge kitchen preparing the gigantic roast of beef, along with heaps of vegetables that were to be their dinner the next day. Suddenly a taxi drew up to the door, and the driver strode in with an immense paper bag, from the top of which protruded two colossal turkey legs.

"It's for you, sir—a surprise."

The missionary took the bird with amazement and turned to his wife. "Well, dear, God must be sending us some more unexpected company for dinner, since this turkey has been supplied."

Scarcely had he made the remark when the telephone rang. He was told that an old, rusty tramp steamer from Japan had just dropped anchor in mid-channel between James Island and Sidney, a few miles from Victoria. To avoid paying dockage fees the ship had anchored outside, and on board were a group of China Inland Mission (Overseas Missionary Fellowship) missionaries released from prison camp in China.

With his usual vigor the missionary threw himself into high gear and contacted the local immigration authorities. After some discussion they agreed that if he personally would stand guardian for the missionaries on board, it would be permissible to take the entire group ashore the next day for New Year's dinner.

Things started to fly in the big kitchen too, as more food was prepared to feed the additional sixteen mouths. There were four children, twelve adults, all of whom had been behind concentration camp walls in China for four years.

Early the next morning the missionary stirred up an old Norwegian fisherman he knew in Sidney. They cranked up the rusty engine of his fishing boat and putt-putted out to the Japanese freighter swinging at her anchor.

Imagine the unbelievable astonishment and delight of those missionaries to find themselves taken ashore for a magnificent meal in a warm, friendly Christian atmosphere. They had not another solitary possession but the clothes in which they stood. All had been lost and left behind in the atrocity of China's prison camps.

If the experience was a moving memorial for the missionaries, it proved almost too much for the servicemen who came to dinner. There they stood in the presence of men and women who, as soldiers in the cause of Christ, had endured four years of terrible privation that surpassed any hardships they themselves had known in combat.

That evening it was suggested by the missionary that as a surprise they phone the daughter of the CIM missionary leader who was a nurse in a hospital in Toronto. She did not even know her folks had arrived on this continent.

"Oh, we couldn't do that!" he protested unbelievingly. "After all, it's three thousand miles away."

"We will anyway," insisted the missionary happily.

He put through the call, and discovered that the daughter had suffered a brain injury, had undergone serious surgery, and was now lying in the same hospital. He requested that an extension phone be run to her room, explaining the circumstances of the case to the hospital authorities. This was done, and in the meantime he set the missionary parents, one at each of the extension lines in his office.

The ensuing scene, with both parents trying to talk at once to their girl, weeping, choked with emotion, was a scene that utterly overwhelmed the strong men in that room. They, too, broke down and wept openly at so touching a spectacle. Ah, the depths of human love and affection, tried in the fires of testing and long separation.

Following this the CIM missionary leader sat back in his chair to recount further the wondrous faithfulness of God to them during the terrible war years in the prison camp. Then he remembered a small book in his pocket and, withdrawing it, began to leaf through its pages. Finally, he found what he was looking for.

The last night they were in China he had gone to the top of a high hill overlooking Hong Kong. There on the summit was a little pagoda with a small circular room overlooking the lights of the city spread below him. Standing on that hill he went back in his mind over the long years in China. He poured out his heart in prayer for this land and its people whom he loved.

As he prayed, he walked around the little room absentmindedly looking at the scribbled names on the walls. All of a sudden his attention was arrested by two Scriptures. Each was written in English, each had under it the signature of Canadian naval seamen. These he marked down in the little black book that rested now in his hands.

He read out the two names and discovered they belonged to two of the very men at this moment in the room with him! So electric was the effect in that place the men could not contain themselves for the powerful emotions that engulfed the group. A petty officer took the missionary aside. "We've got to do something for these folk. Do you mind if we go ahead and raise a fund?"

"Go ahead, by all means," the missionary agreed.

In the quiet, quick way navy men have of getting things done, a splendid sum was soon raised from those present and given to their amazed friends. News of what had happened swept through the city. Gifts poured into the home from Christian friends all over town. One shoe man opened his shoe store and outfitted the entire group with new shoes.

What a day it had been! Such is the wonder of God's eternal

goodness and grace to those who trust in Him. What an example of the good providences of God!

"Oh, the depth of the riches both of the wisdom and knowledge of God! How unsearchable are His judgments and His ways past finding out!" (Romans 11:33 NKJV).

John Calvin: An Arrested Life

BILL FREEMAN

G od by a sudden conversion subdued and brought my mind to a teachable frame."

The sovereignty of God was not merely a teaching to John Calvin; it was his experience. Indeed, his life and ministry is characterized by his being "arrested" by God.

First, he testifies that he was living a life pursuing the will of his earthly father, in changing from the study of philosophy to law, when "God, by the secret guidance of His providence... gave a different direction to my course." Second, Calvin says that while he was steeped in the darkness of Catholic tradition, "God by a sudden conversion subdued and brought my mind to a teachable frame." Third, in relating the account of an overnight stop in Geneva, on his way from Paris to Strasbourg, he says, "William Farel (a zealous French reformer) detained me at Geneva, not so much by counsel and exhortation as by a dreadful curse, which I felt to be as if God had from heaven laid His mighty hand upon me to arrest me." Thus, Calvin's life is an example of how God comes into our lives in unexpected ways to get our attention—to arrest us.

Thank God, He got John Calvin's attention and transformed him into a mighty force in the history of the church for the opening of the truth of God's Word. Calvin was balanced in both the revelation of the Bible and the application of God's truth to a practical church life in Geneva. The work that he did to establish the church life in Geneva was referred to by John Knox, the Scottish reformer, as "the most perfect school of Christ that ever was in the earth since the days of the apostles."

Calvin rarely spoke of himself. His testimony of how he found Christ by a "sudden conversion" has here been pieced together from various sections of his writings:

When I was still a very little boy, my father had destined me for the study of theology. But afterwards, when he considered that the legal profession made its followers wealthy, this caused him to suddenly change his purpose. So I was withdrawn from the study of philosophy and was enrolled in the study of law. I endeavored faithfully to apply myself to this in obedience to my father's will. But God, by the secret guidance of His providence, later gave a different direction to my course.

I had been educated from a boy, always professed the Christian faith. But at first I had not other reason for my faith than what then prevailed everywhere. Your Word, which should have shone on all Your people like a lamp, was taken away, or at least suppressed. And so that no one would long for greater light, an idea had been instilled into the minds of all that the investigation of that hidden celestial philosophy was better delegated to a few, whom the others might consult as oracles. Thus, it was taught that for common people's minds, the highest knowledge suitable for them was to subdue themselves into obedience to the Church. Also, the principles in which I had been instructed were of a kind that could neither properly train me to the true worship of Your Deity, nor pave the way for me to a sure hope of salvation, nor train me correctly for the duties of the Christian life. Yes, I had learned to worship You alone as my God, but since the true method of worshipping was altogether unknown to me, I stumbled at the very threshold.

* * * * *

Compiler's note: Portions of John Calvin's testimony were written by him in the form of a conversation with the Lord.

Jonathan Edwards:
A Miserable Seeking

BILL FREEMAN

T he first instance of that sort of inward, sweet delight in God
and divine things…was a new sense, quite different from anything I had ever experienced."

Jonathan Edwards is known in the history of the church for
the major part he played in the first Great Awakening in America. He succeeded his well-known grandfather, Solomon Stoddard, a Puritan minister of North Hampton, Massachusetts.
Stoddard was a man of God whose life was characterized by a
deep desire to win the lost to Christ, a love for the Word, and
a burden to see the church raised out of its lukewarm state. It
was under this kind of atmosphere and influence that Jonathan
Edwards was brought up.

In his early years, Jonathan Edwards was the subject of much
prayer by his parents. He also had several occasions where he
received "strong religious impressions," but they were only of a
temporary nature. His own testimony reveals that although he
was at times stirred up to pray, it soon wore off and he returned
to his former ways. He admits to going through a period of
"great and violent inward struggles, till after many conflicts with

wicked inclinations, repeated resolutions and self-reflection, 'he made seeking salvation the main business of his life.'" But he describes his seeking as a "miserable seeking."

The contrast between this miserable state and what Edwards experienced when the Lord came into him is seen in his repeated use of the words "sweet" and "sweetness." If we could pick the one word that describes his inner experience of the Lord, it would be the word "sweet."

The following are a few samples of the expressions he used to describe the sweetness he found in Christ: "Sweet delight in God...an inward, sweet sense...sweetly conversing with Christ... so sweet a sense of the glorious majesty and grace of God...many sweet and refreshing seasons walking alone in the fields."

Edwards passed out of a miserable state into a state of sweetness at the time he found the Lord.

Sealed in Safety

EXCERPTED FROM *THE POWER OF* JESUS

A respected Muslim theologian lived with his wife and daughter in the African community. While he was out of town, a *JESUS* team set up a 16mm projector and portable screen in the middle of the street, to enable as many people as possible to watch from both sides. Because of this scholar's position, his wife and daughter were afraid to attend, but rather watched from a distance, just inside the courtyard gate of their home. Fortunately, the volume was loud enough for them to hear—and both received Christ.

When the cleric returned, they told him what had happened. He was furious; he felt they had humiliated him and betrayed Allah. He decided to kill both of them. This man sealed them inside their concrete-walled house, locking the strong doors and windows and leaving them without food or water. He told the neighbors that he and his family were going away and would not return for two weeks. Because of the great distance between the homes, he knew their cries for help would never be heard.

Two weeks later he returned. He unlocked the door, expecting to be hit by the stench of death. Instead, he was greeted by his wife and daughter, both standing before him with joy on their faces. He was incredulous. How could this be? They explained, "You meant to kill us, but Jesus saved us. Every day a hand appeared, giving us food and water. Sometimes it came through the door. Other times the hand appeared through a window. Sometimes it came down from the roof."

The scholar scoffed and refused to believe. Suddenly, the hand appeared and offered him food and water as well. Severely shaken, he immediately went to the local Christian pastor in the community and told him what had happened. The pastor shared the gospel with him. He became convinced that Jesus was the true God, and he prayed to receive Christ.

"For thus the Lord GOD, the Holy One of Israel, has said, 'In repentance and rest you will be saved, in quietness and trust is your strength'" (Isaiah 30:15 NASB).

Before You Call, I Will Answer You

PAUL H. JOHNSON

While I was both praying and fuming, my landscape planner, Carl Johnson (no relation), said to me, "Take it easy. Calm down. Let's see what we can do."

There was a section in the planning ordinance that referred to something called a PUD, or Planned Unit Development. It basically says that if you have ten or more acres of land, you can go to the city with a PUD, and if the city likes it, the officials will, in effect, throw the zoning book away and allow you to build that development only and with that developer only. Carl knew of this and said, "Let me see if we can work something out."

Carl was a fine Christian gentleman and was well liked by the Ann Arbor city officials. He was also an adjunct professor at the University of Michigan and a good friend. We had used him and his firm before.

After a little time, he came up with a plan showing the street going right through the center of our property, just as the city wanted. The plan was to build our project in two phases: 86 units on one side of the street and 156 units on the other side, for a total of 242 units. It was 82 units more than we originally planned. The city thought it was great and issued the permit. We were off and running.

It turned out to be one of our finest projects. Again, the Lord provided things that were above and beyond our expectations. As a future bonus, the city decided to have a city bus come down the street with a bus stop on our property. The bus went by the university and to downtown Ann Arbor, making our apartments a very desirable place to live.

Because we built the apartments in phases, I was able to handle the down payment myself, and I wound up as the sole owner of the project. We did not have any students as tenants except a few grad students, but we had a number of professors and university personnel. We also had a number of retirees.

It was a very successful project. More blessings in my cup.

In All Your Ways

FRANK DIETZ

We had stopped in a little village called Hurriyet in India to get a bite of lunch. Some of the fifteen Indian men on the team handed out gospel tracts as they walked toward the restaurant. While we were eating our rice and dahl we noticed a crowd gathering.

At first, I thought people only wanted to look at my wife, Anneli. Blonde hair and blue eyes were something of a phenomenon in this part of India. We had only been married about two months, and in some ways we were still on our honeymoon.

But subtly the atmosphere in the restaurant changed. Fanatical Hindus were crowding in and a real sense of animosity prevailed. We decided to leave quickly. After paying our bill we went outside and found several hundred Hindus surrounding our five-ton truck, in the act of letting the air out of the tires. Their intentions were obvious. We had almost four tons of Christian literature with us. They would immobilize our vehicle and then burn it.

My first concern was for my wife. I was able to get her into the cab of the truck and the driver—an Englishman and the only other Westerner with us—quickly got us underway. On other occasions when we ran into difficulty, we had always been able to shake off the opposition by the time we reached the village outskirts. But this time, the Hindus chased us. They started with a truck; when they found they couldn't pass us, they switched to an ambassador car. They kept after us for thirty miles, putting up four different roadblocks.

The last barrier was the most dangerous. They had gone ahead to another village and convinced the people there that we were kidnapping some Hindu children. Of course, when they saw young Indian team members among us, this seemed to confirm the story.

At the entrance to the village they had staggered three bullock carts across the road so that when we approached we would have to slow down to go around them. Village people were lined up on both sides, with rocks in their hands. By that time most of the windows in our vehicle, including the windshield, were already broken by previous rocks. The rear tires were in poor condition and likely to blow at any moment. To be honest, it looked to me like the end of the road.

Surprisingly, however, we made it through the gauntlet. Some of the rocks had found their mark, but our adrenaline was pumping and it made us—for the moment at least—oblivious to the pain. A half mile past the village, one of the bad rear tires exploded. We still had one tire on that side so we decided to keep going to the next big city. The car that had been chasing us began to follow, but for some inexplicable reason it stopped. We found out later that it had run out of gas.

Just as we pulled into the city limits of Bellary, the remaining tire on the left side finally collapsed. Our vehicle wasn't going any further, and we felt shaken, physically and emotionally.

Since we obviously couldn't reach our intended destination, we contacted a small Methodist church in Bellary. With their help and the permission of a high-caste Hindu, we set up some tube lights and loud speakers in his field near the city center and started preaching. In India it's very easy to gather a crowd.

Unfortunately a nominal Christian in town decided to try to sabotage our efforts. The first night went well until the Indian evangelist with us started giving an invitation for listeners to accept Jesus Christ. At that point a Muslim magician, hired by our opponent, began making noise and distracting the crowd. When the same thing happened the second night, I jumped off the platform and confronted him. An Indian brother translated and told him that we were doing God's work. If he continued to interrupt God's work he could expect God's judgment.

The next day about three o'clock, a strong wind began to blow. The storm was unusual in its ferocity, tearing down trees and interrupting the power system. The magician's tent, pitched near us, was completely demolished.

When we passed by the next morning, he was cowering in the spot where his tent had been, trembling with genuine fear. He approached one of the team. "Who is your God?" he demanded. In the next days, one hundred people invited Christ into their lives.

But the story isn't quite over. Hundreds of miles north, OM international coordinator George Verwer had come upon two Canadians touring India in a Land Rover. The pair had been planning to drive back to Great Britain, sell the vehicle, and use the money to fly home. The outbreak of a cholera epidemic in Pakistan, however, closed the border to Iran and squashed their plans. When George offered to buy the Land Rover at the price of two air tickets to Canada, they readily accepted.

George didn't have a use for the vehicle, so he decided to send it down to me. He didn't know anything at the time of what we had just gone through. But in the midst of seeing God move in the city of Bellary, we woke up one morning to discover two Indian brothers rolling into the compound with our new vehicle. Needless to say, our hearts overflowed with gratefulness. God's provision, His intervention, and His timing are always perfect.

Peter Rocks: The Second Spiritual Secret

Dick Woodward

I'm so glad that Jesus chose Peter to be one of His apostles. Not only does Peter give a lot of comic relief to the New Testament, he also gives hope to people like me. When I finally came to the end of my rope and admitted that I just couldn't do what God was calling me to do, I began to see that this second spiritual secret is gloriously apparent in the crazy life of the apostle Peter.

Jesus was out walking next to the Sea of Galilee one day. The breeze caught His robe; He shielded His eyes from the sun as He saw two brothers casting their net into the water. They were Peter and Andrew, weathered fishermen who, with their partners James and John, the sons of Zebedee, were about to embark on the greatest adventure imaginable. But they didn't know it yet. (See Matthew 4:18-20.)

"Come," called Jesus, "follow Me, and I will make you fishers of men."

We don't know their entire conversation. Given his personality, Peter was probably annoyed at having his fishing interrupted by some landlubbing rabbi.

But Jesus's words had power. Next thing we know, Peter and his partners in the Zebedee Seafood Corporation were closing down business. "At once," the Bible says, "they left their nets and followed Him."

Jesus was inviting these guys to enter into a relationship with Him. He had just started His public ministry preaching repentance from sin and the coming Kingdom of God. He was telling these two sets of brothers that if they would follow Him, He would make them fishers of *men*, not just fish.

This covenant was essentially a two-part deal. First, "You follow Me. That's your part." Then, second, "I will make you fishers of men…that's My part."

In other words, *"You guys follow Me. That's your business! And I will make you what I want you to be. That's My business!"*

The historian Luke gives us more detail when he records his version of this event (Luke 5:1-11). The brothers had fished for about eight dark hours and caught nothing. At sunrise, while they were tired and frustrated, dejectedly cleaning their nets, Jesus was teaching such a large crowd of people that they backed Him up on the shore of the Sea of Galilee to where Peter was in his boat. Jesus got into the boat so He could have some elevation as He taught.

When the teaching session was over, He told the fishermen to go back out on the water. They were not excited about this idea. It was the wrong time of day to fish. But Peter was starting to figure out that Jesus was God and that he, Peter, was not.

"We've worked hard all night and haven't caught a thing," he told Jesus. (I've always imagined there must have been about a thirty-second pause here when the eyes of Jesus met the eyes of Peter.)

Then Peter said, *"But because You say so,"* I'll let down the nets."

When he did, fish from all over the lake must have rushed

the boat. The big nets overflowed with shining, squirming, silver fish. There were so many that the nets started to unravel from the weight, and Peter signaled his partners James and John (who were in their father Zebedee's boat) to come out for backup. Weighted by tons of fish, the two boats started to sink.

Peter fell at Jesus's knees. "Go away from me, Lord; I am but a sinful man!"

"Don't be afraid, Peter," Jesus responded. "From now on, you will *catch men*." (Those two words are my favorite version of what we call the Great Commission of Jesus Christ.)

Why did Peter want the Lord to go away from him? And why did Jesus tell Peter to not be afraid? Peter was a tough fisherman who'd weathered many a storm. What did he fear?

I think that Peter knew Jesus was recruiting him for a radically different life. Like me, he was afraid to be changed, afraid of the ministry. I'm convinced that Peter was saying to Jesus, "You don't want somebody like *me* doing that! I can't do that! I'm a sinful man! I swear sometimes! I'm a mess! Go away from me!"

Peter needed to understand that if he was going to "catch men," it wasn't really up to him. The night before, Peter couldn't even catch fish. He *certainly* could never catch men until he learned to say, *"I can't, but He can!"*

Jesus was the Fisherman, not Peter. And Jesus knew what Peter could not yet see: that in just three years, after Jesus's crucifixion, resurrection, and return to heaven, Peter would preach a sermon so full of power and truth that three thousand Jews from all over the world would become charter members of the New Testament Church. As Peter observed the supernatural happenings of Pentecost, in that anointed sermon he proclaimed that Jesus was the risen Christ "having received from the Father the promise of the Holy Spirit, He poured out this which you now see and hear" (Acts 2:33 NKJV). Peter knew who the Fisherman was on the Day of Pentecost.

Throughout the explosive growth of the church, this rough and clueless fisherman would be the means by which multitudes would come to faith. He would do actual miracles. Right up to the moment of his martyrdom, Peter proclaimed that Jesus was the one doing the miracles and bringing the human fish into his spiritual net. He knew that he could do nothing, but that Jesus could do everything.

I'm no Peter. But when I began to see the reality of the second spiritual secret, my life, like Peter's, changed forever.

Miracles of the Power of Jesus

All glory to God, who is able,
through his mighty power at work within us,
to accomplish infinitely more than we might
ask or think.

Ephesians 3:20

Miracles of the Power of Jesus

When we think of the power of Jesus, our thoughts usually focus on His creative and sustaining power over the universe (Colossians 1:15-17). It is so much more than that! The apostle Paul said, "I am not ashamed of this [gospel] Good News about Christ. It is the power of God at work, saving everyone who believes—the Jew first and also the Gentile" (Romans 1:16).

His power is activated through the prayers of believers, conviction of the Holy Spirit, and presentation of His Word—the Bible. People everywhere are waiting to hear the good news.

Rebelados

EXCERPTED FROM *THE POWER OF* JESUS

In the mountains on the Republic of Cabo Verde, an island country spanning ten archipelago islands off the coast of West Africa, sit a number of isolated villages where approximately three thousand people have lived in self-imposed isolation. These villages, founded by escaped slaves during the era when the island of Santiago served as a slave processing post, developed and grew as more and more slaves escaped over the years. Due to the remote mountain locations of these villages, the colonial powers at that time left them to function on their own. Following Cape Verde's independence in 1975, these communities refused to be part of the new independent country and continued to maintain their social isolation.

They call themselves "Rebelados" (Rebels). They raise their own food and live in houses made from cornstalks. They do not use modern machinery or ride in cars. They refuse to take part in the national census, elections, or national health care. They do not allow their children to attend school.

Cape Verdean pastors tried to visit the Rebelados over the years, but each time they approached the villages, the children emerged and viciously threw stones at them until they retreated.

Due to this self-isolating practice of stone-throwing, the Cape Verdean churches have been unable to evangelize these villages.

The Rebelados worship an old Spanish Bible that a Spanish priest gave to an escaped slave. Unable to read, they do not understand the message of this book. Hence, many Cape Verdean pastors prayed for many years for a gospel outreach to the Rebelado people so that they might understand the message of the book they worship.

During the Easter season of 2011, the *JESUS* film was shown for the first time in Kabuverdianu-Sotaventu, the mother tongue of all the people on the island of Santiago. When Noel Alves, a retired Nazarene pastor, received a copy of *JESUS*, he decided to take on showing this version of the film as his full-time ministry. Converting an old van into a mobile film-showing unit, he travels to remote rural areas and to the mountains where he sets up camp to show the film. He reports that people walk for miles to see the film, and many are coming to know the Lord.

Following a showing in a remote village, a man approached Pastor Noel saying he had walked fifteen kilometers to see the film. This man asked Pastor Noel to show the film in his village. Pastor Noel went with him to his village, where he discovered the man was the chief of the Rebelado communities and a descendant of the slave who had been given the Spanish Bible.

The chief heard that *JESUS* told the story of the book they worship, and he wanted his people to see and hear the message in their language. Pastor Noel stayed with the Rebelados for three days. He showed *JESUS* in three parts each evening and gave a follow-up message after each part. During the day he visited the villagers in their homes to share more about the message of their Spanish Bible.

Those who prayed for years for the Rebelados are moved to tears when they reflect on how the Lord answered their prayers by using the *JESUS* film, in the language of the Rebelados, to clarify and illustrate the message in their Spanish Bible. Since this showing the Rebelado communities have opened up to the work of the Cape Verdean churches, and many other pastors have been able to visit. Translated Scripture portions have been introduced, so the Rebelados can begin learning to read, in their own language, the message of the Spanish book they worshipped throughout their history.

A Special Kind of Love

JOSH MCDOWELL

I had a lot of hatred in my life. It wasn't something outwardly manifested, but there was a kind of inward grinding. I was disgusted with people, with things, with issues. Like so many other people, I was insecure. Every time I met someone different from me, he became a threat to me.

But I hated one man more than anyone else in the world: my father. I hated his guts. To me he was the town alcoholic. If you're from a small town and one of your parents is an alcoholic, you know what I'm talking about. Everybody knows. My friends would come to high school and make jokes about my father being downtown. They didn't think it bothered me. I was like other people, laughing on the outside, but let me tell you, I was crying on the inside. I'd go out in the barn and see my mother beaten so badly she couldn't get up, lying in the manure behind the cows. When we had friends over, I would take my father out, tie him up in the barn, and park the car up around the silo. We would tell our friends he'd had to go somewhere. I don't think anyone could have hated anyone more than I hated my father.

After I made my decision for Christ—maybe five months later—a love from God through Jesus Christ entered my life and was so strong it took that hatred and turned it upside down. I was able to look my father squarely in the eyes and say, "Dad, I love you." And I really meant it. After some of the things I'd done, that shook him up.

When I transferred to a private university I was in a serious car accident. My neck in traction, I was taken home. I'll never forget my father coming into my room. He asked me, "Son, how can you love a father like me?"

I said, "Dad, six months ago I despised you." Then I shared with him my conclusion about Jesus Christ: "Dad, I let Christ come into my life. I can't explain it completely, but as a result of that relationship I've found the capacity to love and accept not only you, but other people just the way they are."

Forty-five minutes later, one of the greatest thrills of my life occurred. Somebody in my own family, someone who knew me so well I couldn't pull the wool over his eyes, said to me, "Son, if God can do in my life what I've seen Him do in yours, then I want to give Him the opportunity." Right there my father prayed with me and trusted Christ.

The Man in the Clouds

EXCERPTED FROM *THE POWER OF* JESUS

Some years ago, in India, a young national missionary couple felt the call of God to take their three-year-old son to a very resistant area in the north to live among the Malto people. They labored faithfully for many years in this notorious area known as the "graveyard of missionaries" without seeing a single person come to Christ. Their every effort to share the gospel was met with opposition as they battled discouragement, depression, spiritual oppression, and polluted water. One day the husband walked through the door of their tiny home, collapsed, and died.

A few weeks later, a *JESUS* film team arrived in that exact Maltos area. This time the government officials allowed the film to be shown. During the scene at Jesus's baptism in the Jordan River, when His face first appeared on the screen, the crowd erupted with shouts and exclamations. The team had no choice but to stop the film and learn what the commotion was about. "It's the Man!" they shouted. "He is the One we saw walking in the clouds!"

It seemed that everyone had seen Him the day the national missionary died. Clouds formed over the hillsides. The vision of a Man, larger-than-life, appeared above the clouds—walking over their hills, shedding tears. The Malto people suspected that it was a message from God, that He was displeased that they had rejected the gospel.

Now, they were being given a second chance. As the team restarted the projector, the people settled down to continue watching the film. Everyone was transfixed by the story. Then, at the end, the majority of these hard, resistant Malto people put their faith in Christ!

Other miracles followed. People were delivered from evil spirits. The sick were healed. The deep spiritual hunger of many was met.

But the greater miracle is this: Where once there were no Christians, there are now forty-six thousand Malto believers and hundreds of growing and maturing churches! Today they are preparing to send out their own missionaries to other unreached people, some who will use the *JESUS* film. The "graveyard of missionaries" has become the "vineyard of missionaries"!

An End Which Was a Beginning

Excerpted from *The Power of* JESUS

A *JESUS* film team traveled to a harsh prison that housed some of the most violent offenders in this African country. The team asked the warden for permission to show the film. Because he was devout in his religion, he adamantly refused.

The team suggested that Jesus could bring peace to his prison—that showing *JESUS* would help change hearts. Their arguments must have been appealing because he changed his mind. They set up the projector and screen as the prisoners, mostly murderers, rapists, and thieves, filed in. Most had never heard the gospel.

At the end of the film, many indicated a desire to trust Christ. The response was so great that the team asked the warden if they could show *JESUS* again later. They also boldly asked if they could establish a New Life Training Center (NLTC) in the prison, so they could continue to help new believers understand the Scriptures.

A graduation ceremony for those who completed the NLTC training was held, with one thousand inmates in attendance. With shackles around their wrists and ankles, the graduates went forward to receive their certificates. Each gave a testimony of how Jesus had radically changed his life. That night, forty-seven more prisoners surrendered their lives to the Lord, twenty-seven who were from Muslim backgrounds.

One of the shackled men was to be executed five days later. On the day of his execution, a *JESUS* film team member (who had helped him experience the power of the Word expressed in the film) came to encourage him. As he climbed the steps to the gallows, this condemned man did not stop praising God and singing. He declared, "Outside I was a murderer; I killed three people and I would have killed again. But in this place I found Christ. And my whole family has now been saved."

The inmates and prison guards were stunned by his calmness and joy. As the rope was placed over his head and with a smile on his face, he told his executioner, "The moment you pull the lever, I will be with Christ."

Manobo Girl Delivered from Demons

Tom Lyman

I spent many years as a missionary in the Philippines. One day a young man came to the house asking me to go with him to Datu Wata's house. It seems that one of his daughters had become demon possessed. It took four or five men to restrain her, and she was incoherent.

When I arrived I could see the young girl writhing, being constrained by some of the men. I tried to speak to her, but there was no communication. I asked what had happened, and the family told me the story.

This particular day the family had gone to the rice field to do some weeding. The young girl did not want to go so she was told to stay in the house and not go out. This is a custom, especially regarding young single women, for fear of the evil spirits. But during the day she became thirsty, so she went out to the spring to fetch some water. As she was filling her water jug, she heard hideous laughter, and she ran for the house in fear. But as she was entering the house she felt a warm kind of feeling enter her body, and from that moment she evidenced the symptoms described above.

This was a first for me, and I was very uncertain about what to do. I finally prayed over the girl, demanding in the name of

Jesus Christ that the spirit come out of her and leave her alone. Of course I was hoping for a dramatic change in the girl, but nothing happened.

I learned later that soon after I had departed, the girl returned to normal and fell into a deep sleep. She slept the day through, as well as the night.

700 Terrorists on the Ground

Excerpted from *The Power of* JESUS

Bruce and Jan Benson, longtime missionaries in Peru, are partners who frequently showed the *JESUS* film. This time the location was in a village high in the mountains. After witnessing the power of God's living Word to change the hearts of people, the Bensons left rejoicing.

But, unwittingly, they were driving directly into the hands of terrorists. Bruce carefully negotiated the narrow mountain road, deep in the Andes. Coming over a hill, they pulled to a stop just behind a seemingly stalled truck.

Instantly, scores of rifle barrels were thrust in their direction by a band of radical Maoist terrorists, known as "Shining Path" guerrillas. The Bensons were taken back to the village. The forty-five heavily armed terrorists proceeded to interrogate and threaten the Bensons and the townsfolk.

Before they released them, the terrorists went through their belongings. They found and confiscated all the projection equipment, intending to use it to show revolutionary films. Out of frustration, Bruce also handed them the film reels saying, "Here, you may as well take these too," silently praying, "Lord, do not let Your Word return void."

A year later, back in the city, Bruce received a visitor. One of his captors had become a Christian! It was a man named José, a seasoned Shining Path terrorist who had killed many people in cold blood. Bruce listened as José told his incredible story.

> The day we captured you, we intended to kill you. But each time we talked about it, something stopped us. After we released you and returned to our camp in the jungle, we were bored and began to watch the film. At one point there were seven hundred of us on the ground before the screen. We saw that Jesus was a true revolutionary. Many in the movement were so moved by His life that they wanted to lay down their arms and leave then.

He told Bruce how he subsequently had been arrested and sent to jail, and gave his life to Christ. He then asked Bruce to forgive him.

José is now a pastor and the director of a major Bible school in Argentina. He is also actively sending out missionaries around the world!

The Strange Exchange:
The Third Spiritual Secret

DICK WOODWARD

Okay, as I said, the real reason I didn't put together the Mini Bible College material was my lack of self-discipline.

I just plain didn't want to spend the time it would take to write that comprehensive Bible overview. I wanted to run and run and run. I wanted to meet with people, speak at prayer breakfasts, appear on television, and talk to people in bars about Jesus—all great things, of course. But they weren't what God was specifically calling me to do, and in pursuing them instead of the Mini Bible College, I was being disobedient.

You remember the biblical story of Jonah? Like me, Jonah was obedience-challenged. God told him to go preach to Nineveh, the capital city of Assyria, the greatest enemy Israel had. This was like asking a Jew in the early 1940s to go to Berlin and preach against the evils of the Nazis.

So it was understandable, humanly speaking, that Jonah basically responded by saying, "I don't want to." I wouldn't have wanted to either.

Jonah seems to have forgotten just who he was dealing with. He tried to run away from God. He got on a ship headed the opposite direction, as far from Nineveh as he could get, according to the maps of the day.

God, being God, didn't lose track of Jonah. He caused a huge storm to engulf Jonah's escape vessel. The pagan sailors were so petrified that they became believers. Jonah told them to toss him into the sea, apparently preferring to die rather than obey God.

God sent a creative rescue vehicle, a huge fish that swallowed Jonah like he was a dose of plankton. Swishing around in the digestive juices for seventy-two hours, Jonah decided to agree with God. The great fish burped, and Jonah became sea monster vomit. That was a tough way to learn a good lesson.

As you know if you read the short book of Jonah—which is worth reading, believe me—our hero went to obey God. He still didn't want to go to Nineveh, but he knew that God wanted him to go. So Jonah went.

He was probably quite a sight, bleached and smelling like God-knows-what from his inner tour of the big fish. I'm sure he raised a few eyebrows and offended a few noses in Nineveh. But then the cruel, skeptical, pagan people of that great city repented of their great evil and turned to God.

Incredible!

God has given us, like Jonah, the freedom of choice. In a sense, He won't make us do anything. But He will put us in the belly of a huge sea monster until our only reasonable option is to choose to obey. Our lack of desire is overcome. Like Jonah, we can learn the third spiritual secret: *I don't want to, but He wants to.*

It's a strange exchange, one that gives us a life-defining sense of mission, vision, purpose, and freedom. God gives us His ability in exchange for our disability. He gives us His will when we give Him ours.

The Bible puts a huge emphasis on the alignment between our will and the will of God. Jesus's greatest prayer was, "Not

My will, but Your will be done." He taught us to pray, "Your kingdom come. Your will be done in earth—or in our earthen vessels—as it is in heaven."

God will not violate our freedom of choice, but He loves us enough to lean on us like an elephant until the only reasonable choice we have is to do His will. I am of course not suggesting that any physical suffering in this life is a "punishment" from God for disobedience...far from it. We can't know the mysteries of why God allows illness and suffering. All I know was that in my particular case, God cut me back physically so that I might bear more spiritual fruit.

My advancing disability meant that I could no longer run and run and run. Yet God was calling me to realize my dream. I had experienced in my life that *"I'm not, but He is,"* as well as, *"I can't, but He can."* Now I was actually ready to learn God's will—His *"want to"* could turn around my *"want to."*

Through my severe limitations, God was making me an offer I could not refuse. He wanted to show me that it was time for me to do some things for Him the way He wanted them done. He didn't toss me into the digestive tract of a large fish, but He fastened my bottom to a wheelchair.

As a result, I had plenty of time to work on my Bible course. We had moved to Williamsburg by this time and the church there was very gracious with my time. For the next five years, I was able to devote forty to sixty hours a week to developing the Mini Bible College. We held services twice on Sundays, had a midweek service, and I spoke at two men's Bible study breakfasts during the week, but my preaching and teaching flowed out of the intense Bible study—a complete Bible survey for laypeople—that I was writing. It equipped people with powerful truths for living as followers of Jesus.

The night before His crucifixion, Jesus connected with His apostles in a way that shaped their souls forever. Talking with them in the garden, He took hold of a vine with branches that were filled with clusters of fruit. You guys are like these branches, He told the apostles. My Father, the Gardener, prunes branches so they can produce even more fruit.

Two thousand years after Jesus taught His apostles that truth I could see its tender yet painful process in my own life. I was a branch needing a significant cutback. He pruned me, if you will, so He could work miracles in me and through me. He had plans I couldn't have dreamed of. This may sound sanctimonious, but it's true: Today, I don't consider my paralysis as a setback. It's a cutback, the tough but loving action of a loving Heavenly Father, designed for my good and for the greater good of many others.

Isn't it intriguing how God works? Even when we try to run away from His will, He will find a way to motivate us to get the job done. Maybe that's true in your life. Maybe you feel like Jonah, trapped in the intestinal tract of a large sea creature. But you're not trapped. Don't think God can't get you where you need to be.

Simple Miracles

The miracles of earth are the laws of heaven.

Jean Paul

Simple Miracles

Now that's an oxymoron! All miracles are incredibly complex since they, by very definition, are supernatural interventions!

But in my research I ran across stories that seemed on the surface to be less spectacular and more commonplace. That raises the question of the amount or even commonness of miracles in the lives of Christians. I believe that in the effort to select miracle stories that are spectacular, we miss the simple, little, or even common miracles we encounter each day. So, at the risk of equating incidents with miracle happenings, I included a handful of "simple" miracle stories to balance the spectacular with the common in life.

Kicking the Habit

John Van Diest

We were a typical rural farming family—Dad and Mom, my brother and sister, and me. We lived on a hundred-acre dairy farm near the Skagit River in northwest Washington. It was near a little town called Lyman. Dad was tough and Mom was more than a cook, helping twice a day with milking more than fifty cows as well as many of the other chores associated with making the farm profitable during the waning years of the Great Depression.

Mom and Dad chose this obscure location because of the attractive purchase price of $10,000, but also prompted by their desire to escape the religious "obligations" of attending church in the Dutch community of Lynden, a town with many Dutch and Christian Reformed churches. While in the Lyman area they had "religious freedom," even though there was a small Baptist church at the edge of town pastored by Rev. and Mrs. Edwin Swanson.

Almost like clockwork, every month an American Missionary Union worker would drop by the farm and seem genuinely friendly to Dad. Every morning we three kids would board the rural bus for school—our driver also pastored the local Baptist church. He also showed genuine interest in our family. As a re-sult of these relationships, each of our family of five came to faith in Christ.

Dad struggled with his new role of being a Christian parent, but over time he managed to grow. One of his habits was his addiction to smoking. He "rolled his own" and puffed about a pack a day. He tried many times to quit but was not able to kick the habit. Soon it became a spiritual struggle. They prayed and prayed that his desire for cigarettes would go away.

In the midst of the struggle and prayer, one day Dad desired to smoke but found it painful because his mouth was covered with sores. These sores provided the time needed to quit. As a young twelve-year-old, the events were his struggle to stop smoking, and then due to sores—or was it a miracle answer to prayer?—he was able to quit, which caused my own faith to be greatly strengthened.

Both Mom and Dad are now in heaven. But I'm still amazed by how God used a faithful pastor in an obscure town in the northwest corner of the United States to befriend a farmer and his family and lead them to faith in Christ. Dad, who had not even finished grade school, sold the farm and moved our family to Chicago to attend the Moody Bible Institute. While there, he worked at the Chicago United Mission, giving him a desire to work with the homeless. After returning to the West Coast (so each of us kids could attend Multnomah University), Dad started the Portland Rescue Mission, which today serves hundreds of men and women caught in addiction.

My brother Gale, after graduating from university, served as a missionary in Alaska and eventually became the Mission's di-rector. Each of their five children is active in service to the Lord. My sister, Fae, served Christ as wife and mother of three, volun-teering in many Christian service areas through the church and working at Multnomah Press, a Christian publishing company, along with her husband. Two of her children work for churches.

I was privileged to serve as publisher of Multnomah Press. My wife, Pat, and my children are all active in Christian service. Several of our grandchildren are in training for Christian service in various Christian colleges and universities.

The key (real miracle) in this family story was two critical decisions made by our parents: first, to accept Christ as Savior, and second, to respond to His call for kingdom service. Clearly, each of the individuals mentioned in this story are "plain Jane" and "average Joe" types of people. No superstars here, yet generations have been brought to Christ.

In many ways, the motto *"Only one life will soon be past, only what's done for Christ will last"* is worth pursuit.

We Have Been Waiting for You!

EXCERPTED FROM *THE POWER OF* JESUS

A deacon of a large church had a vivid dream. Before him he saw a familiar street in his large city, and a house address 269. The following night he had the same dream. When he awoke, this strong believer felt he should investigate, believing his dream could be from the Lord.

The deacon went to the street, found the address, and knocked on the door. A man with a white robe, beard, and turban—a religious leader and teacher—answered and invited the deacon in. He found himself in a room filled with more men in white robes and turbans, all sitting in a circle...and women covered head-to-foot in their burkas. Nervously, he accepted the robed man's offer of tea, sat down, and chatted. To talk about Christ in their presence could cost him his life, so he soon got up to leave.

On his way out the leader inquired, "But, why did you come?" Hesitantly, the deacon replied, "I had a dream. I saw your street and your house number. So I came, believing God sent me here." The leader replied, "We have been waiting for you! We have all become followers of Isa (Jesus) and have been praying that God would send someone to tell us more about Him. We gather here secretly because we cannot talk about our faith outside this room. You must come again. There are many more groups like us in the neighborhood, meeting secretly in houses. You must also tell them more about Isa (Jesus)!"

Charles Spurgeon: A Seeking Heart

BILL FREEMAN

Look unto Me!...I had been waiting to do fifty things, but when I heard that word, 'Look!' what a charming word it seemed to me!"

Charles Spurgeon was raised in a godly home in England. Both his father and grandfather were ministers of the gospel. At the age of ten, he began to seek God regarding his own salvation. After a period of about five years, he happened to attend a Primitive Methodist meeting in which the passage, "Look unto Me, and be ye saved," was being preached. That day Spurgeon found Christ.

Soon Spurgeon himself began to preach. He was so effective that by the age of nineteen this "boy-preacher" was attracting large crowds in London to hear the gospel of Christ. He continued preaching in that city, primarily at the Metropolitan Tabernacle, for thirty-eight years until his death in 1892. The following, taken from his book *Autobiography*, gives an account of the day he found Christ.

> I sometimes think I might have been in darkness and despair until now had it not been for the goodness of God

in sending a snowstorm one Sunday morning while I was going to a certain place of worship. When I could go no further, I turned down a side street, and came to a little Primitive Methodist Chapel. In that chapel there may have been a dozen or fifteen people. I had heard of the Primitive Methodists, how they sang so loudly that they made people's heads ache; but that did not matter to me. I wanted to know how I might be saved, and if they could tell me that, I did not care how much they made my head ache. The minister did not care how much they made my head ache. The minister did not come that morning; he was snowed up, I suppose. At last, a very thin-looking man, a shoemaker, or tailor, or something of that sort, went up into the pulpit to preach. Now, it is well that preachers should be instructed; but this man was really stupid. He was obliged to stick to his text, for the simple reason that he had little else to say. The text was—

"Look unto Me, and Be Ye Saved,
All the Ends of the Earth!"

He did not even pronounce the words rightly, but that did not matter. There was, I thought, a glimpse of hope for me in that text. The preacher began thus: "My dear friends, this is a very simple text indeed. It says, 'Look.' Now lookin' don't take a deal of pains. It ain't liftin' your foot or your finger; it is just, 'Look.' Well, a man needn't go to college to learn to look. You may be the biggest fool, and yet you can look. A man needn't be worth a thousand a year to be able to look. Anyone can look; even a child can look. But then the text says, 'Look unto Me.' Ay!" said he, in broad Essex, "many of ye are lookin' to yourselves, but it's no use lookin' there. You'll never find any comfort in yourselves. Some look to God the Father. No, look to Him by-and-by. Jesus Christ says 'Look unto Me.' Some of ye say, 'We must wait for the Spirit's workin'.' You have no business with that just now. Look to Christ. The text says, 'Look unto Me.'"

Then the good man followed up his text in this way: "Look unto Me; I am sweatin' great drops of blood. Look unto Me; I am hangin' on the cross. Look unto Me; I am dead and buried. Look unto Me; I rise again. Look unto Me; I ascend to heaven. Look unto Me; I am sittin' at the Father's right hand. O poor sinner, look unto Me! Look unto Me!"

When he had gone to about that length, and managed to spin out ten minutes or so, he was at the end of his tether. Then he looked at me under the gallery, and I daresay, with so few present, he knew me to be a stranger. Just fixing his eyes on me, as if he knew all my heart, he said, "Young man, you look very miserable." Well, I did, but I had not been accustomed to have remarks made from the pulpit on my personal appearance before. However, it was a good blow, struck right home. He continued, "and you always will be miserable—miserable in life, and miserable in death—if you don't obey my text; but if you obey now, this moment, you will be saved." Then, lifting up his hands he shouted, as only a Primitive Methodist could do, "Young man, look to Jesus Christ. Look! Look! Look! You have nothin' to do but to look and live." I saw at once the way of salvation.

Taking Time Out

PAUL H. JOHNSON

After developing many apartment complexes, all of which were doing quite well, we developed a small strip center in Southfield with about twenty stores. It became a legacy for our three kids. We built a few other buildings for other people, but mostly on a cost-plus basis. We weren't very aggressive about seeking new work. We just did what came our way.

With all the properties producing a steady income, I was forty-one years old and had enough income to retire—except that I had to manage the properties, which was much less stressful than developing them. I figured I was about halfway through my productive life, with twenty years behind me and maybe twenty years ahead of me. And maybe it was time to reevaluate my life and see if the Lord had something different for me to do with the rest of my life. Maybe we should get away from the business for a while and just sit down, pray, meditate, and give the Lord time to give me some direction. At that point the business could just about run itself. Also, we had a desire for our three children to be in good Christian schools, and there were none in our area.

So we bought a home in Ft. Lauderdale, Florida, and took our small boat and a few personal things and moved. The home was furnished. We put our three children—Colleen, fifteen; Kevin, thirteen; and Karen, eight—in Christian schools. Colleen went to a Christian prep school near Orlando. I returned to Detroit for a few days each month for meetings, etc. We lived there for an entire school year.

After all the Bible reading, praying, and meditating, I received no word, no message, no indication of any changes I should make in my life. So we sold the house and returned home. My mom and dad had lived in our house while we were gone. One indication for us to return was that our church started a Christian school, and we enrolled Kevin and Karen in the opening year. Colleen was still in a Christian school near Orlando, Florida, where she was in high school.

The year we lived in Ft. Lauderdale was interesting. We had heard of the Coral Ridge Presbyterian Church and Dr. D. James Kennedy. It was their Christian day school that Kevin and Karen attended. We started attending the church and became acquainted with "Jim," as he told us to call him.

His daughter, Jennifer, also attended the school. She was in the same class as Karen. They became good friends. With last names that started with J and K, they were often seated together. After a while, Jennifer was at our house or Karen was at their house one or two nights a week. We became good friends with Jim and Ann Kennedy.

Jim had come to Ft. Lauderdale to establish a Presbyterian church. It was like a missions church. He started with a very small group and eventually saw it grow to a very large church with a well-known television program. The reason for the growth was largely due to a ministry of evangelism. The church grew because of new believers. If anyone visited the church, someone from the church would call on them in their home. They were encouraged to ask two basic questions. First, they would ask, "If you were to die tonight and stand before the Lord tomorrow morning and

He asked you, 'Why should I let you into My heaven?', what would you say?" Most responses were something like, "Well, I think I have been a pretty good person. I think I am better than a lot of people. I never killed anyone. I've been a good husband or wife..." and so on.

Then the visitor would ask, "Just how good do you think you have to be to qualify for heaven?" Most people didn't know what the standard was. Many said there is no way to know until you get there, and God will decide. Then they would ask, "Don't you think that's kind of scary to go through life not knowing whether or not you are going to heaven?" Many would say, "I just don't think about it."

Then the question was asked, "Wouldn't you like to know for sure that you were going to heaven?" As you might guess, many would say, "Sure, but how can that be?" at this point the visitor would share with them the basic gospel message—that it's not what we do; it's what Jesus Christ has already done. All of us are sinners from birth. Everybody has done something wrong. No one is perfect or deserves heaven, which is a perfect place. So God, knowing that, sent His Son, Jesus, to pay the price for our sin by dying on the cross. All we have to do is acknowledge that and, by faith, trust Him; and the by-product is eternal life in heaven.

Most people would say, "It's that easy?" With a simple prayer of confession and sincere belief, the Bible, God's own Word, says we are made clean before God and become His children with the gift of eternal life. It is not what we do. It is all by faith!

As you might guess, many people prayed that prayer and began attending the new church where they were fed spiritually and their faith began to grow and become stronger. As a result, the church grew and grew with new believers. In fact, Jim wrote a book called *Evangelism Explosion*, and many churches used the program to train their people how to simply share the gospel with others.

* * * * *

One person who was a member of the church has a fascinating story of God's love.

A group of five guys played cards every Friday night. They played at their different homes. Sometimes the game would go on until two or three o'clock in the morning because they didn't have to work on Saturday. One night they got carried away, and the game went on until 5 a.m. When they finally finished, one of them said, "Why don't we all go out for breakfast?" Then someone reminded him that most restaurants didn't open until 6 a.m.

Sort of in jest, one of them said to the fellow in whose home they were, "How about you wake up your wife and ask her to make breakfast for us?" He said, "Are you kidding? She would kill me." Another one said, "You know, I bet if Bill called his wife, Ann, she would get up and do it for us." Another one said, "Are you kidding?" as he looked at Bill. Bill said, "Yeah, she probably would." He said, "I don't believe it. I dare you to call her."

So Bill went to the phone and called his wife and asked her if she would make them breakfast. She said, "Okay. Give me about forty-five minutes and come on over." They did, and as they walked into Bill and Ann's house, they could smell the bacon frying and the coffee brewing. They all sat down to a lovely complete breakfast.

As Ann was pouring additional coffee, the skeptical guy said, "Ann, I have to ask you a question. What on earth would make you get up at five o'clock in the morning and serve a bunch of bums like us such a lovely meal?"

With that, she put the coffeepot down and walked over beside her husband, Bill. She put her arms around his shoulders and said, "You know, Bill here is not a believer in Jesus Christ. Therefore, he is not going to heaven to enjoy all the benefits that God has promised for us for all eternity. The only joy and pleasure that he will ever know is what he experiences in this life. I love him very much, and therefore I want to do whatever I can to make his life here on earth as comfortable and happy as I can, because it's the best he'll ever know." With that, the table went silent. Finally, Bill said, "That's just the way she is."

The story has a good ending. Bill plus two others became believers in Jesus Christ because they saw demonstrated a life that reflected the love for people that can only come from having a proper relationship with Him! Ann's actions for an hour or so were so unusual and unnatural that they spoke volumes to those guys about real love, more than a four-hour lecture or an entire book on the subject. Remember: "Nobody cares how much you know until they know how much you care!"

"You Are the Ones! You Are the Ones!"

EXCERPTED FROM *THE POWER OF* JESUS

A *JESUS* film team traveled to a remote area in Central Asia, to a country that borders the Caspian Sea. It's a place where many hazards await Christians who openly declare that Jesus is Lord. The team ventured into the unknown, trusting God with the outcome and their safety. En route, they lost their way. They stopped in the middle of nowhere, hoping to reestablish their bearings, when a man surprised them—suddenly emerging from a cluster of trees. He was agitated, waving his arms over his head and heading directly for them.

The team was obviously concerned. Why was anyone out this far alone? Was he insane? Could he be a threat? The man drew closer, shouting at them excitedly. *"You are the ones! You are the men in my dream! Can you give me Truth?"* Standing there, miles from any settlement, he told them about his dream several nights earlier. He had seen men coming to him. He heard a voice saying that they would bring him Truth. The dream captivated him...it was so real. He had left his home on foot and been searching for them since, and he recognized them as the very men in his dream!

The *JESUS* film team invited him into their car, and he gladly directed them to his village over the dirt roads. It turned out he owned the local teahouse—the place where all the men of the community would gather. That evening the team showed them *JESUS* in their language. The man and his whole household became followers of Christ!

"The Spirit told me to go with them without misgivings… And he reported to us how he had seen the angel standing in his house, and saying, 'Send to Joppa and have Simon, who is also called Peter, brought here; and he will speak words to you by which you will be saved, you and all your household'" (Acts 11:12-14 NASB).

A President Paves the Way

STEPHEN HART

The riverboat wasn't much to look at. According to locals, the vessel had sunk twice and burned once. But our team decided that if it could stay afloat for the two weeks they needed it in late December, it would do. Their dream of mounting an exhibition of Christian books in Khartoum, the capital of Sudan, was about to come true.

Besides renting the boat, the team reserved and paid for a mooring on the busy side of the Nile River, right next to a main roadway in the town center. What a place to reach the crowds! But when they steamed up, the local officials refused to let them come in. "Too shallow," was their excuse. Disconsolate, we were forced to withdraw to the opposite side of the river where far fewer people passed by. *How will we ever draw people here?* they wondered. They prayed and asked the Lord for help.

And God answered—*with a landslide*! A quarter of a mile up the river, a stretch of the bank slid down into the Nile, washing out the footpath. The president of Sudan himself went to inspect the damage, accompanied by a military escort and TV cameras. While he was there he noticed a boat moored a little further down the shore. Strings of lights decorated the vessel and loudspeakers blared music and messages. "What's this?" the president wondered. He and his party sauntered over for a look, with TV cameras following.

When our "motley crew" saw the military delegation approach they were sure it was the end of everything. But an officer introduced them to the president, and they were pleased to give him a "royal" tour, crowning it with the presentation of a Bible. The president appeared greatly pleased and kissed the Bible— gesturing respect for a holy book, and conveying his response that he accepted the gift with pleasure.

The TV cameras recorded everything, and that evening all the viewers in Khartoum watched it on their screens. The next morning a photograph of the Bible presentation was splashed on the front pages of leading newspapers. For days afterward, the boat was swamped with visitors! The team not only saw a huge sale of Christian literature in Arabic and English, but they had scores of friendly conversations with the local populace. Before the two-week event was over, at least five visitors professed faith in Jesus Christ. Thanks to a mudslide, they didn't miss the boat!

Just a Jackass: The Fourth Spiritual Secret

Dick Woodward

One November morning when the Thursday morning men's breakfast was at its peak, an international banker stood up to say a few words. "As we approach Thanksgiving this year, the thing I am most thankful for is Dick Woodward—because I have found Christ at this breakfast!"

When I came up next to teach, the whole audience of men rose and gave me a long, standing ovation. I was grateful, but embarrassed too.

I'm not hot on the jackass stories in the Bible. Remember the account of Jesus's triumphal entry into Jerusalem? Jesus was riding on the back of a donkey, and people were all around Him, spreading palm branches on the path in front of Him. They shouted, "Blessed is He who comes in the name of the Lord! Hosanna!" Providentially, that very week I had heard a world-famous Presbyterian radio pastor ask the question, "When all those people were shouting all those wonderful things about Jesus, now wouldn't it have been silly for that little old jackass to think that was all for him?"

So after all those men stood and applauded at that breakfast,

I shared what I had heard on the radio, and then I said, "If the Lord has spoken to you here, or if He has ridden into your life through this breakfast, thank HIM. Don't thank the jackass!"

Even though I knew the donkey shouldn't get the acclaim, it took many more years for me to fully grasp the truth of the fourth spiritual secret: *"I didn't, but He did!"*

Like all secrets, it's absolutely freeing. It's not about us; it's about God. When He brings fruit in our lives, or when He does miracles and great things of any kind, we can't take the credit. We didn't do it. He did. We can be free to be humble and truly God-honoring. It would be pretty ridiculous for Jesus's donkey to think people were cheering for him. The same is true for us.

The apostle Paul was no jackass. He was probably the Bible's most credentialed achiever. He was pretty relentless about his résumé. He was a triple-A personality who had faultless credentials and a track record full of good works. After he came to faith in Jesus, God utterly converted his soul but maintained Paul's personality and gifts, using them for a new purpose. Paul wrote half of the New Testament and put the Church of Jesus Christ on the world map. He pressed himself to do all he could for the kingdom of God.

It would have been easy for Paul to fall into the trap of pride. While he wasn't perfect in his post-conversion life, he knew full well the power of the fourth spiritual secret.

In his inspired letters he writes, continuously and emphatically, that it was not he who did these great things. He wrote to the Corinthians that when he preached the gospel and planted the church there he did so in great weakness, in fear and much trembling. He claimed that his ministry there was a demonstration of the power of the Holy Spirit. In his writings he consistently conveys, "I didn't, but He did." He ran his race full tilt, knowing that any fruit of his work came from the power of God, not from the power of Paul.

Miracles of Healing

Jesus never met a disease he could not heal,
a birth defect he could not reverse,
a demon he could not exorcise.
But he did meet skeptics he could not convince
and sinners he could not convert.

Philip Yancey

Miracles of Healing

Can God heal? Sure. Does God heal today? I think so. There are just too many credible reports of healing for us to deny them.

Biblical examples give some clue to His purpose in healing. John the apostle is clear that the purpose of healing the blind man was to show the power of God. Jesus apparently raised Lazarus from the dead for several reasons: to show His power over death, to demonstrate His Messiahship, and to show compassion to Mary and Martha.

Then, too, there is that amazing passage in James 5:14-15 that says the elders are to be called to pray over the sick. And this, mixed with faith, can lead to healing. No doubt this promise is a key to healing miracles.

Bend Down, O Lord

Terri Justice

I'm not sure you could even call it a prayer. It was more of a fleeting thought or a wish I would mutter to the Lord as I watched my husband's health decline. The first miraculous kidney transplant my husband, Mike, had brought us much joy and celebration for the first few months following surgery. Yet soon after that it became laden with troubles, ups and downs, followed by a gradual loss of function. We knew that a transplant is not a cure, just a form of treatment. Oh, but we were so hopeful!

If Only

After seven years hanging on to his partially working kidney, Mike went back on the transplant list. "Lord," I said desperately to Him in the quietness, "if only I could do something." I'd see Mike tired with the fatigue of anemia that accompanies poorly working kidneys. I'd see him unable to eat foods he enjoyed or not hungry at all as the kidney failed to clean the toxins out of his system. "Lord, what can I do?"

One day as we talked about what might lie ahead for us—dialysis, declining health, possibly the inability to work—I said once again, "Honey, I wish I could give you one of my kidneys." To me it was a sincere wish, yet just beyond my grasp. Several factors have to match between donor and recipient, and for us, nothing matched. Not even our blood type. I am 0-positive and Mike is B-positive.

Good News

I traveled to Alaska to visit with my sister for a few weeks, and while there I called home to check on Mike. "I have some good news," he said.

I knew he had been to the transplant clinic for a checkup, but surely he wasn't gaining kidney function back. Nothing had pointed to that.

"They are starting to do spouse-to-spouse transplants now," he said. "It's called 'Living Unrelated Donor.'" The new medications were so good that even without a close match, they seemed to prevent rejection of the transplanted kidney.

Surprised, I felt a spark of excitement inside. "Should I request an application for you?" he asked.

"Sure! Let's get going on this."

I returned home with hope that I could actually do something to help. The rest of the summer included doctors' visits, psychological evaluation, a battery of medical tests, and meetings with social workers and surgeons. At the end of all the investigation, we found that I passed with flying colors as a candidate to donate a kidney to Mike. The transplant committee finally approved our request and set the date for our surgeries.

God heard my wee prayer, my wish, my desire, and in His wondrous way He made it possible. Several years ago surgeons removed my left kidney and placed it into my husband. It began working immediately, doing the job his kidneys could no longer do. It was our miracle!

"Bend down, O LORD, and hear my prayer; answer me, for I need your help...For you are great and perform wonderful deeds. You alone are God...With all my heart I will praise you, O Lord my God. I will give glory to your name forever" (Psalm 86:1,10,12).

God Is Enough

GREG KERNAGHAN

When we were crisscrossing cultures by sea and land on the *Medical Voyage (MV) Doulos* and *MV Logos*, my wife Anni and I were privileged to see God's hand at work in many ways. Our lifestyle created a high degree of corporate dependence on God's merciful intervention, and it was natural to speak of our hope being "God or nothing." Yet it was a different test entirely when we faced our greatest personal crisis.

Having lost our first child through a miscarriage, our excitement, nervousness, and hope grew perhaps faster than the new child we awaited in the spring of 1983. Anni's first six months of pregnancy passed without event. Then, on a rough voyage from the Faroe Islands to Bergen, Norway, serious problems suddenly arose. Anni had to be hospitalized. The following day *Logos* sailed on to its next port of call. I stood on the quayside, feeling absolutely alone.

But God had foreseen everything and His plans were already in motion. I was introduced to a local Christian family who was willing to host us for as long as necessary. This was not just any family, for I learned that six years before, the couple had gone through the identical experience that we were now entering. Their daughter was born in the same nearby hospital, one of the finest university research facilities for premature babies in Scandinavia. The six-year-old's lively presence gave me hope.

The diagnosis, however, was not encouraging. Both Anni and the child within were in grave danger. The doctors' priority was to prevent the toxic effects of preeclampsia and other complications from causing permanent liver damage to Anni. Her blood pressure rose to dangerous levels.

Tests showed that the child, approaching twenty-eight weeks, had not grown in two weeks. The umbilical cord was wrapped twice around his neck. The pregnancy had to be terminated.

On May 19, our son Jaakko was removed from his mother's womb and whisked away to the Premature Intensive Care Unit where he would spend the next eleven weeks. He was given a 10 percent chance of survival with no regard to normal development. He weighed only nine hundred grams and was thirty-seven centimeters in length; my hand formed an ample cradle.

I rushed to Anni's side, but she was not yet in the mood for guests. So I returned to see "my son"—that phrase tasted good! There he lay in an incubator, so covered with wires and tape and monitors that he was nearly hidden. I instantly realized why he could have used another three months in the womb. Besides being tiny he had no fat whatsoever; his skin tore like paper when sensors were changed.

He spent eleven days on a respirator, which bloated his abdomen like a frog. Milk was pumped into his stomach round the clock. Every biological function was scrutinized. None of this made him seem real. I hovered near him, afraid even to touch him.

I will be forever grateful to the wise doctor who saw my reaction. "Wash your hands and pick him up," he instructed. "He's your son and you both need each other."

I cannot describe the transformation that followed. The tiny fist that instinctively grabbed my finger became, to me, an invitation to place this child in God's keeping. Whatever the future held, we were one and that could not be taken away!

Anni had not been able to experience this vital bonding, for she had not yet seen Jaakko. She was not recovering as the doctors had hoped. Ten days after his birth I was thrilled to be able to take her to "meet" him, hold him, and weep in joy over him. Her own recovery accelerated from that moment.

Jaakko's eleven weeks in Intensive Care were unquestionably the most intense period of my life. Our visits were the focus of each day. Whenever Anni and I weren't with him, the ringing of the telephone made us sick with apprehension.

But strangely, neither Anni nor I tried to demand healing or life, either for her or our son. At that flash point of faith when we felt that everything we leaned on was being stripped away, we still knew that we loved God deeply and wanted to please Him, come what may. God Himself was all we really would ever need.

We also discovered that, in the heat of crisis, one quickly runs out of ways to pray and is reduced simply to watching and waiting. Our own hearts were so overwhelmed we could not carry the burden any longer. But we knew with certainty that a prayer network spanned the globe, interceding for us. To this day, I still meet people who have never met Jaakko and yet feel they know him because of their prayers.

There were several tense moments during those weeks and, in fact, for the first two years in Jaakko's life. Yet there remained a strong conviction on the part of many friends that God had a purpose for Jaakko's life. I have never forgotten that.

Two years later, our daughter was born under similar, yet less threatening, circumstances. Maria weighed eighteen hundred grams, which is tiny to most people but twice as large to us! Good things *do* come in small packages! Today Jaakko and Maria are "normal" teenagers and we are likely "normal" parents of teenagers. But we are still awed whenever we remember God's goodness and touch upon our lives.

You Matter: A Message from Nathan

PAM VREDEVELT

If the greatest commandment is to love God and love others, then Nathan was one of God's greatest gifts to our family. He taught us to slow down and love. He mattered.

Nathan's big sister, Jessie, writes about the vision she had March 3, while Nathan lay in the Intensive Care Unit, two days after his accident.

My little brother, Nathan, was in a coma, on full life support, in the pediatric ICU at Emmanuel Hospital. Two days earlier, a car barreling 55 mph down the freeway hit him full force. The devastating impact caused severe brain injury, multiple broken bones, and other vital organ damage. Our family stayed with Nathan around the clock. We held his hand, stroked his arms, sang of God's goodness, and talked to Nathan about how much we loved him.

It was a bizarre turn of events. One minute we were in the Moda Center arena cheering the Portland Trail Blazers, our favorite basketball team, to victory. The next we are rallying groups to search the grounds for Nathan. I had given him permission to use the bathroom inside the suite our friends had invited us to enjoy. While waiting behind two other people in line, he quietly slipped out of the suite, into the foyer crowded with half-time spectators. Nathan never did understand the implications of wandering. He was a special child, born with Down syndrome, who loved wild adventure. This particular night, he set out on another exciting escapade that led to his exit from this world.

My mind replayed the accident over and over like a broken record. I didn't want to close my eyes for fear that I would relive the horrific scenes in my dreams. Anguish surged through me as I imagined Nathan running onto the freeway, disoriented by the dark of night, terrified by car lights speeding toward him. The thought of Nathan being all alone in unspeakable pain was more than I could bear. God knew this and met me.

It was an encounter like no other. I don't dream dreams or see visions. But this particular night God opened my eyes to see into the invisible realm. It was like a curtain had been pulled back. I saw the rear of the ambulance surrounded by black night. The doors were open wide. Light was streaming from inside. But it was empty. Nathan wasn't there. Instead, he was sitting on top of the ambulance next to Jesus beaming with joy. They were playfully kicking their legs back and forth, arms wrapped around each other's shoulders, completely enthralled in each other's love.

Suddenly I saw a close-up of Nathan's face. He looked like Nathan, but there was no trace of Down syndrome. He was radiant. He was healed, obviously thrilled to be with his best friend. The playful smile on his face said, "I've got a secret, Nana (his nickname for me). I know something you don't know, ha-ha!" That was Nathan! He loved to tease.

Next I saw Jesus and Nathan watch the EMTs recover Nathan's body from the pavement and place it into the ambulance. In seconds the picture disappeared and an all-consuming peace silenced my torment. God met me in my darkest moment. I knew without a doubt, Nathan wasn't scared. He wasn't in pain. And he definitely wasn't alone.

Let Nathan's story be a reminder: YOU MATTER!

Precious Seed

DEBBIE MEROFF

When little Danielle Shugart died with lightning sudden-
ness from acute leukemia in June of 1990, a huge chunk
of the Shugart family's world came crashing down. During their
four years in Pakistan, they had fielded a great many of the enemy's "flaming arrows." A couple of years before, they survived
the explosion of an ammunition dump near their house. This,
the death of a beloved child, was hardest of all.

Ten months later, they celebrated the birth of another
daughter, Sophia. Craig and Krista Shugart's joy, however, was
immediately shadowed by anxiety.

"I don't think it ever crossed our minds, or at least settled in
our hearts, that we were disadvantaged or ripped off. There was
some fear as implications for the future set in, but in the midst
of it God gave us satisfaction in what He had done. Sophia's
birth improved the quality of our lives. We don't minimize the
difficulties, but we don't let ourselves get bogged down in them."

After Sophia's birth, Craig continued teaching math and
chemistry in a private school in Pakistan. The next year he was
offered the prestigious post of headmaster of a major boy's high
school.

But Satan was ready with yet another unexpected assault. Craig developed a lesion in one ear that was diagnosed as a malignant melanoma: skin cancer. This type of melanoma is rare— and fatal unless they catch it in time. The doctors felt they had. The only treatment is to cut off the affected skin tissue. "They told me that if another lesion ever appeared it meant the cancer had invaded internally and there was no hope," he remembers.

Some months later, another lesion did appear. Although it seemed futile, Craig was immediately scheduled for surgery. Friends around the world prayed. And something totally inexplicable—by medical standards—occurred. When he reported to the doctors in Canada for the appointed surgery, they discovered that the lesion had disappeared. There was no trace of the melanoma.

The Shugart family was happy to return to Pakistan. Life was not easy. Krista had to work hard with Sophia, helping her with special programs. But according to Craig, God gifted her with a great love for children and an appreciation of what "quality of life" really means.

"We still miss Dani," he admitted. "Hardly a day goes by that the family doesn't recall her, that she's alive with God. But the Lord actually gave Krista a premonition before she died. He spoke through the verse, 'Unless a kernel of wheat falls to the ground and dies, it remains only a single seed. But if it dies, it produces many seeds' (John 12:24 NIV). The Lord told Krista clearly that Dani was that seed. She was our 'down payment' for the work in Pakistan. We can't walk away from that."

A Miracle-Working Church

CARL LAWRENCE

"Many wonders and signs were taking place" (Acts 2:43 NASB).

To ask a participant in the house church in China whether or not he is experiencing things that might be classified as unusual for believers is to invite a quizzical reply: "I don't know what you mean by 'unusual.'"

"Well, you know, things a little strange...things that don't happen every day."

"You mean miracles?"

"Yes...yes, I guess that is what I mean. Yes, that is what I mean...miracles."

"You mean healings?"

"Yes, healings...you know, like Mr. Huang."

Mr. Huang was a worshiper of Buddha. His health began to deteriorate until he could not keep any food in his stomach at all. After a thorough examination, the doctor diagnosed his case: "You have a cancer of the liver and are at the terminal stage. There is nothing we can do for you."

Mr. Huang returned to a small town near his native village to await the inevitable. While there, he heard about a doctor in the town and decided to get a second opinion or perhaps obtain some medicine that could prolong his life. This doctor was a Christian. Later, this doctor would accompany Mr. Huang as he gave his testimony. The Christian doctor confirmed the first diagnosis as cancer of the liver in an incurable, terminal stage.

The Christian doctor told the man that there was no medicine that could prolong his life, but that if he would believe in Jesus Christ, he could have eternal life. He carefully explained the gospel to Mr. Huang and urged him to believe on the Lord Jesus Christ. The doctor also explained that Jesus was the Lord and had the power to heal any sickness if it was His will. "But whether Jesus heals you or not is not important," the doctor said. "What is important is that you have eternal life."

"I want to believe in Jesus," Mr. Huang said. The doctor called in another Christian man, and the three of them knelt in his office as Mr. Huang became a new person in Jesus Christ.

Returning to his home, he told his wife of his faith in Jesus Christ and asked her to remove all the idols from their house and burn them. She did as she was told. She knew her husband's condition was hopeless. From then on, Mr. Huang's condition deteriorated rapidly.

Every night, he and his wife knelt and prayed together. He thanked the Lord that whatever happened to him physically, he now had eternal life. He was gripped by terrible pain. His wife fixed some food.

Over the next weeks, he became so weak that the family began preparations for his funeral. The coffin was purchased, and the grave dug on the hillside.

One night a man in a white robe appeared to him in his sleep. The man was holding a knife. Not knowing what he intended to do, Mr. Huang struggled with the man, but the man prevailed and touched Mr. Huang with the knife. He awoke the next morning at eight o'clock and was hungry for the first time in many days. After eating a nourishing bowl of egg-drop soup, he fell asleep.

After some time, he awakened, and saw two men in white robes standing by his bed. "You have been healed," they said. He reached down and found all the pain and swelling gone. Being extremely hungry, he ate a hearty meal. When his brother came to pay his last respects, he was amazed to see him sitting up and strong. He told his brother that Jesus had touched him during the night and he was completely healed.

This event can be attested to by several of his coworkers and a Christian medical doctor who has witnessed patients being divinely healed. The miracles that are common in the house church in China are varied. All, however, are for the glory of the Lord. All the attendant benefits, such as giving comfort to the grieving, are also present.

King of Hearts

Alfy Franks

During the 1970s we had a man with a great burden to work for God in north India. At one point this man, Nelson George, fell ill and became increasingly weak. Doctors examined him and sent him to a cardiologist. This specialist afterward called Ron Penny, who was then the leader of the work in Bihar where Nelson was. He told him that Nelson was very seriously ill and probably had only about ten days to live. His heart was so enlarged there was nothing medical science could do for him.

Ron did not tell Nelson, only suggested that he go home and take a month's rest and see the doctors there. Nelson went home, traveling almost three days by train. The second cardiologist told him to return after another three days, when he had had sufficient time to rest from his long trip. Then, he said, he would start Nelson on some medication.

Nelson was so weak at this point that his church was alarmed. Members began to fast and pray. When we in Bombay heard the news that Nelson had an enlarged heart and Ron Penny revealed the seriousness of his condition, we also fasted and prayed continuously. After three days, Nelson went back to see the specialist.

The doctor was stunned by Nelson's obvious improvement.

He kept looking at his patient as though he were a ghost. Then he examined him. The evidence was indisputable.

Later, he admitted that when he had first seen Nelson he doubted that he would live beyond another ten or so hours.

"That is why I told you to come back after three days. I felt there was no point in examining you when it was so apparent that you were not going to live for very long. Why go through all the hassle of medications that were not going to do any good?"

"God has definitely healed you," stated the cardiologist simply.

To Nelson the news was no great surprise. Medical science had its limitations, but God knew all about human hearts. There wasn't one the Lord couldn't heal in answer to His children's prayers.

Open My Eyes, Lord!

Stella Chan

I was serving aboard the *MV Logos* when we sailed the South China Sea and rescued more than eighty Vietnamese "boat people." Some of the refugees suffered from fever, eye disease, or skin disease. This added a big burden to our ship's medical team, which was run by a doctor and a nurse. I was planning programs with the ministry department, but by profession I am a registered nurse and midwife. I was glad to use my free time to help on the medical side. However, I never dreamed that I would become a patient myself!

I was sharing a cabin with Joy, an American woman. One night I was awakened from sleep by sharp pains in both my eyes. I could not open them, so I used my fingers to pry up my right eyelid. The pain increased in intensity and tears poured down my face. I was shocked, realizing that something was seriously wrong. Quietly I cried out to the Lord, asking for His help.

It was the middle of the night. Everyone was sound asleep, and I had no idea what I should do. I determined not to waste my pain. I knew my Master must have a lesson in this and asked Him to teach me whatever He wanted me to learn. In my heart I started to sing songs to praise and thank Him for His love and

His suffering for me on the cross. I told Him He was the Lord of my life, and thanked Him for the thirty-two years I had been able to use my eyes. I said that I was willing to accept whatever He decided was best for me, knowing His grace was sufficient.

When Joy woke up and saw me she was alarmed—each eye had swollen to the size of an egg!

The ship at that time was tied up in Bangkok, Thailand. Dr. Chong, the ship's doctor, tried to go ashore and find an eye specialist, but he was unsuccessful. "Stella, I honestly do not know what's wrong with your eyes. The eye pressure is normal. Let us pray, and I will put in some eyedrops and try some medicine."

He applied the medication, and we prayed. I know the whole crew prayed as I lay in my bed during the next days, feeling physically exhausted. I could not open my eyes and lived in the dark. Still, my heart rested upon my God.

On the second evening our captain came to visit me in my cabin. He told me that Dr. Chong's medical report said my eyes were in critical condition. With a firm but gentle voice he asked, "Stella, do you believe in prayer for healing, and shall I pray for you?"

I assured the captain that I would welcome his prayer. He knelt down on the floor beside me and put his hands on my eyes. Then he spoke a few simple words, asking the Lord to touch me.

And that's exactly what God did. For the first time the next morning I was able to open my eyes. They were still very red, however, so I whispered another prayer.

"Lord, I know You've touched me. Can You please let my eyes return to the proper color in three hours' time? If they do I can attend a meeting that is important for the ministry on board."

Every half hour I looked anxiously into the mirror to see if there was a change. Just before the meeting was due to start, my eyes cleared!

When I left the *Logos*, in my autograph book Dr. Chong

remarked upon our "very interesting experiences" together. Then he added, "Remember your swollen eyes? I am surely glad that our Lord is the sovereign God—and that you got well, in spite of my treatment."

So am I, dear Dr. Chong! Neither of us ever doubted what made the difference, when human help was not enough. It was the touch of the Master.

Everyday Miracles

God did not place you on this earth
to notice Him at work only once or twice in
your whole life.

Bruce Wilkinson

Everyday Miracles

When we get to heaven, I believe we'll be surprised just how many miracles happened to us while we were on earth. If you have a guardian angel(s), and the Scripture indicates you do, then it's just possible, if not probable, that you experience miracles more often than you think!

Miracles are designed and performed for God's special people...those who, by faith, have become Christians. Therefore, miracles are not limited to "super saints," but each of us is a candidate for miracles.

The Mountains of Iran

Joe Aldrich

In a village in the mountains of Iran, a number of new believers heard that they could find out more about Jesus if they could get the book of the Christians called the Bible. One night, a man had a dream that if he went down to the highway, some men would come by who would give him a Bible.

The next day, he gathered a little offering of money from among the believers in the village and made his way down the mountainside to the highway that ran through the area. He sat on a rock and began to wait.

Sometime later, two men in a car just "happened" to pick up a shipment of Bibles across the border. They were driving along this highway when the steering on their car suddenly locked. They couldn't move it more than an inch.

They finally nudged the steering wheel just enough to get the car over to the side of the road. They put up the hood to figure out what was wrong. A man sitting on a nearby rock called out to them, "Are you the men with the Bibles?"

Stunned that this man should know, they admitted, "Well, yes, we do have Bibles." The old man gave them all the money he had collected, bought as many Bibles as he could, and made his way back to the village. The men with the Bibles then went back to determine what was wrong with their car, but could find nothing. They shrugged their shoulders, got in, and drove away.

Are You an Angel?

BRUCE WILKINSON (REWRITTEN BY JOHN VAN DIEST)

My friend Bruce suggests in his book, *You Were Born for This*, that we should daily ask God to arrange the circumstances to open opportunities to serve Him. As an example, he tells the story of an encounter he had while driving late at night. He came upon an older model van off the side of the road with a man wearing a turban, waving for help! For those of you who know Bruce, he has a tendency to help anyone who seems to be in trouble.

The man indicated that his van had broken down, and he was without cash, a requirement of the tow truck he needed. He had been there for hours, dripping with perspiration and worry!

After inviting him into his car and giving him a bottle of cool water, Bruce learned he not only had spent hours in the heat, but he had tragically been verbally abused with profanity by several people who drove by. He was worried that his wife and kids were no doubt panicking by his long overdue arrival at home.

At that point Bruce believed this was God's answer to his earlier prayers! He apologized for all the inconsiderate people who passed like the Pharisees in the Good Samaritan story (Luke

10:29-37). Bruce asked the man to forgive those thoughtless people and then gave him more than enough money to pay for the tow truck. In keeping with his pattern of helping people in trouble, when the man assured Bruce he would pay him back, Bruce refused and said he had money "set aside" to give whenever God indicated to give it.

The man was flabbergasted and did not know what to say. Then it dawned on him that Bruce might be an angel—which Bruce assured him was not the case. The man realized that Bruce was sent by God!

Bruce has a great desire to represent God daily. His generous spirit was exhibited to me once when we were in Los Angeles ready to fly home—he to Atlanta and I to Portland. He said, "Hey, John, mind if I fly to Portland with you?" While most likely he had many other friends in Portland where we both served on the faculty of Multnomah University, he said he just wanted to spend time talking! In flight, he asked a somewhat familiar Bruce-ish question: "What can I do for you, John?"

Hannah W. Smith: A Discovery of God

Bill Freeman

It was a plan of salvation that I could understand…it was all the work of Another done for me."

Hannah Whitall Smith's book, *The Christian's Secret of a Happy Life*, is a spiritual classic and has helped countless Christians understand the true nature of the Christian life. Hannah, along with her husband, Robert Pearsall Smith, is also known for founding the famous Keswick Convention for the cultivation of the "higher Christian life."

Hannah's personal discovery of God came after a process of searching that began with what she called "the aching void in my heart." This aching void was temporarily satisfied by the aid of a teacher named Anna. Anna spoke to her of giving up all to the Savior, but she did not show Hannah the way, except to admonish her, "Let us struggle for a portion of His Spirit."

Because of this kind of inner realization, Hannah was feeling deep desires for God but did not know how to find Him. Thus, she was plunged into a period that she called "morbid self-introspection." Her daily cry became "How do I feel?" not "What does God say?" She characterized her relationship with God at that time as being based on how she felt toward God, not on how God felt toward her.

After being in this state of introspection for a few years, Hannah was driven into skepticism for a period of two years. She then went through a season where she was "cold and dead again and full of pride!" Her idol was "the pride of human reason," and she confessed that she was about to speak out her skepticism and doubts to others when an event took place that changed the whole course of her life. She tells about this event in her own words, revealing how she found Christ.

> It was in the year 1858 and I was twenty-six years old, and my heart was aching with sorrow. I could not endure to think that my darling had gone out alone into a godless universe; and yet, no matter on which side I turned, there seemed no ray of light.

> It happened just at the time the religious world was being greatly stirred by the inauguration of daily noonday meetings held from twelve to one, in the business part of the city [Philadelphia], and crowded with businessmen. I had heard of these noonday meetings with a very languid interest, as I thought they were only another effort of a dying-out superstition to bolster up its cause. However, one day I happened to be near a place where one of these meetings was being held, and I thought I would go in and see what it was like. It was an impressive thing to see such crowds of busy men and women collected together at that hour in one of the busiest parts of the city, and I remember wondering vaguely what it could all be about.

> Then suddenly something happened to me. What it was or how it came I had no idea, but somehow an inner eye seemed to be opened in my soul, and I seemed to see that, after all, God was a fact—the bottom fact of all facts—and that the only thing to do was to find out all about Him. It was not a pious feeling, such as I had been looking for, but it was a conviction—just such a conviction as comes to one when a mathematical problem is suddenly solved.

One does not *feel* it is solved, but one knows it, and there can be no further question. I do not even know that I heard anything. A tremendous revolution was going on within me that was of far profounder interest than anything the most eloquent preacher could have uttered. God was making Himself manifest as an actual existence, and my soul leaped up in an irresistible cry to know Him.

It was not that I felt myself to be a sinner needing salvation, or that I was troubled about my future destiny. It was not a personal question at all. It was simply and only that I had become aware of God, and that I felt I could not rest until I should know Him. I might be good or I might be bad; I might be going to heaven or I might be going to hell— these things were outside the question. All I wanted was to become acquainted with the God of whom I had suddenly become aware.

When Contacts Matter

Don Hillis

In February of 1955 Francis Schaeffer was informed by the Swiss government that he and his family were to be out of Switzerland within six weeks. The reason given was that they had a religious influence on the Champery community where they lived.

Imagine with me, if you can, the deep challenge to faith this ultimatum brought to Dr. and Mrs. Schaeffer and their three daughters and infant son, Franky, who had been stricken with polio a few months previous to this. But these servants of the Lord had faced hard obstacles before and they knew others would pray with them.

Along with their praying, they wrote letters and made phone calls to contacts that might prove profitable. Godly friends whose lives had been blessed through their ministry did the same. Among these contacts was a visit to the American Embassy in Berne.

There, to Dr. Schaeffer's delight, he found that the senior consul had been born in Philadelphia, had gone to Germantown High School, and had graduated in 1930. That was Schaeffer's identical story. Needless to say, they spent a happy few hours as ex-classmates reminiscing. Though the American consul promised to do what he could to help, he was in no position to tell the Swiss government what they should do with their expatriates. This happy experience was, however, an encouraging reminder to Francis and Edith of God's thoughtful providences even in little things.

In the meantime, appeals were being made to the Chief of the Bureau des Etrangers to reverse the expulsion order. As a result, the Schaeffers were informed that they would have to find a house in another canton, in a village in which the officials would welcome them and would be willing to make an appeal to Berne. Several days of cold and frustrating chalet hunting followed. Though those days carried their share of discouragements, they also carried some God-honoring contacts.

Then, on the last day before the chalet needed to be obtained, Edith met a real estate agent who encouraged her to go with him to Huemoz to a chalet. It was just right, but there was a catch. It was not for rent; it was for sale! From whence would so much money come?

Undaunted, Mrs. Schaeffer returned home to break the news. When she arrived there she learned that the Swiss government had extended the time they could stay in Switzerland. However, the local canton insisted they must be out of the village at the previously scheduled time.

That night there was specific prayer for the supply of $1,000 before ten o'clock the next day. The next morning the mail delivered to them consisted of three letters. One was from a couple in the States whose lives had been quickened through Dr. Schaeffer's messages. Three months before sending this letter to Switzerland they had discussed investing money in a house they could rent out. But now they had decided to send it to the Schaeffers toward the purchase of a house that could be used for the ministry to young people. The enclosed check was for

$1,000. This was answered prayer in the very deepest sense—at just the right time.

A decision to take the chalet was made. The down payment was 8,000 Swiss francs (about $2,000 at that time). The Schaeffers' money on hand was 8,011 francs. What a large and meaningful step forward this was. However, the final permit to remain in Switzerland still had to be obtained.

It "just so happened" that two maiden ladies lived in the house next door to the Schaeffers' new home. They "just happened" to be the sisters to one of the Swiss government's Council of Seven that rules the country. He was one of the alternating presidents of the country and at that time was the president. On hearing of the Schaeffers' plight, they phoned their brother and informed him of the situation. This was plainly not a coincidence. The living, personal God of the Bible had arranged it.

Two doors away on the other side of the Schaeffers' home lived an elderly, white-haired pastor. When he heard the story about his new neighbors, he at once wrote a letter to his nephew. Can you guess who his nephew was? He was the head of the Bureau des Etrangers in Berne. The ultimate signing of the permit for the Schaeffers to stay in Switzerland would be in his hands. A few days later the maiden sisters reported that all was well. The expulsion order would be rescinded. On June 21st the passports were returned with the word "ANNULE" stamped over the evacuation order.

Source: Don W. Hillis, *God, You and That Man with Three Goats!*, p. 47. Don is a missionary statesman and past president of the Evangelical Alliance Mission.

A Korean Houseboy

Paul H. Johnson

During the Korean conflict, a fifteen-year-old Korean boy helped the American soldiers in their barracks, doing things like laundry, cleaning, shining their shoes, etc. The soldiers called him a "houseboy." One army sergeant took a liking to him and nicknamed him "Billy." Since almost everyone in Korea is named Kim, they called him "Billy Kim."

His life is a story of its own. It is most remarkable how the soldier got Billy to America and helped him get a college education in a Christian university. After marrying an American girl named Trudy from Pontiac, Michigan, Billy and Trudy went back to Korea as missionaries. During his college days, he met two brothers from Toledo, Ohio—Wall and Gus Yeager. They were the sons of Waldo Yeager, a friend who got me involved with Winona Lake.

Waldo became very impressed with young Billy Kim and wanted to help him and Trudy with financial support as they went back to Korea as missionaries. He formed a new ministry called Christian Service. It was registered with the IRS and was a tax-exempt organization. Waldo asked me to be one of five or six board members. I agreed.

Billy had a phenomenal ministry in South Korea. He started a church and began to hold evangelistic meetings all over the country. In fact, after a while, he became better known in South Korea than Billy Graham was in the United States. His personality and reputation were amazing. He was, and is, one of the most respected individuals in South Korea.

One time when he and Trudy came to the United States for a visit, there was a reception for them. Some of Trudy's family attended, and I was introduced to her younger brother, Herb Stephens. We had a nice visit.

Sometime later, out of the blue, Herb showed up at my office. He said he had a problem. Herb owned several mom-and-pop-type motels all along I-75 from Pontiac, Michigan, to Sault Sainte Marie in the Upper Peninsula. His problem was that he purchased a motel in Pontiac on a land contract and he was behind in his payments. If he didn't pay $40,000 by Friday, he was going to lose the motel.

I looked over the situation, and it was obvious that it was worth more than $40,000 so I loaned him the money with a recommendation that he get a long-term mortgage and pay off the land contract holder. He insisted that I become his partner in the motel business. I really wasn't interested, but he gave me 50 percent interest anyway.

A little while later he got a mortgage and paid me the $40,000. I thought that was the end of it all. A year or two later, he showed up again at my office. I thought, *Oh, no. He wants to borrow some more money.* Instead, he said, "Guess what? I sold the motel." I said something like, "Good for you." Then he told me to sign some papers, and when he closed the deal, he would bring me my portion of the proceeds.

So I signed. A few weeks later he came back with a check for $75,000. After I thanked him, I went back into my office and I remember just sitting there all alone and looking at the check and thinking, *This is a gift from God! I really didn't do much to deserve this. So let's put it to work with Billy Kim. They are missionaries in Korea. That's the connection. Let's send it to them.*

I called Billy in Korea and told him that I had just come into some extra cash and asked him if he had any need for it. He said, "In fact, we do." He explained that they were building an "old folks home." He said there were none in Korea at that time and that there was a great need to care for the elderly. When I told him "Okay," he asked me how much I had. I said, "$75,000." There was a long silence on the phone. I finally said, "Billy, are you still there?" He said in a very weak and broken voice, "Yes, I'm still here." He went on to say that $75,000 was exactly the amount they had been praying for, as that was what was needed to finish the project. I said, "Okay. The money will be on its way to you tomorrow." That was maybe thirty or forty years ago. The project was finished, and they called it the Paul and Marilyn Johnson Old Folks Home.

But the story doesn't end there. About five years ago, I got a phone call from Billy in Korea. He said, "Guess what? We sold the old folks home." I said, "What? You sold the old folks home?" I asked him how much he got for it. He said, "$9 million." He said the location had become very strategic and valuable, and BMW, the German company, wanted to build their new headquarters to serve all of Korea on the property.

When I asked Billy what he was planning to do with the $9 million, he said they were going to go out in the country, where land was less expensive, and build a new bigger and better multilevel old folks home. In November 2012, Pam and I and Colleen and Drew got a tour of the building with two towers— one wing for the patients who can still walk around and one wing for the ones who are bedridden. The main floor houses the chapel, dining room, and other facilities. It is a lovely structure and well used to ease some of the pain and suffering that comes with old age. It is amazing how God makes *much* out of a *little* when we let go and let Him have control!

Bull's-Eyes!

BOB GRIFFIN

My friend Nate Saint once said, "Landing our little missionary airplanes on jungle airstrips is like parking in the garage while driving 60 miles an hour." I've parked in a lot of those garages.

The Hohulins are Bible translators working with people who speak the Ifugao dialects in the mountains of the northern Philippines. Their airstrip was a jim-dandy—for them. It cut a grueling two-and-a-half-day hike to a twelve-minute flight. But for the pilot it was something else. The 490-foot airstrip had been chiseled precariously into the side of a steep mountain ridge. One end was a very solid, nearly vertical basalt mountain; the other, a cliff, instantly supplied two thousand feet of stomach-wrenching altitude on takeoff. Parking in Hohulin's garage was always an experience!

Early one morning I made three trips to get Dick and Lou and all their gear out for a linguistic workshop. After the third landing I had a few moments while I waited for Dick, so I walked back to the approach end of the strip. Like any marksman, I wanted to check the target, to see where I had touched down on each of those three "adrenaline generators."

Bull's-eyes! All three were bull's-eyes! Every touchdown was within fifteen feet of the others and about one airplane length from the end! I was really tickled.

Not bad, I thought, mentally patting myself on the back. And well I could. I'd have patted any pilot on the back for that. I knew it required considerable skill. It wasn't misplaced pride, just satisfaction in a job well done. I'd been practicing for a long time to acquire that skill.

All this came to mind recently when I was reading the story of David and Goliath. I have read that story since I was a kid, but I had never thought much about David's skill with the sling and his confident assertion to Saul that he could do the job. I guess I'd always taken his victory for granted and assumed that God gave David especially good aim when he really needed it. Now I realize how foolish that was—as foolish as assuming God would suddenly give me good aim to spot-land the Helio Courier on a short, scary airstrip in the mountains. I'd guess that David had pegged more than a few stones at various and sundry targets!

Bull's-eyes don't just happen. David was a good marksman because he practiced.

When I was a boy on the farm, I just about wore out the .22 rifle my father gave me. I shot that gun so much I hardly ever missed. I even got good enough to toss up a little clod of dirt and leave it a puff of dust in the air. That's pretty good shooting.

I wonder if David ever tried that? Maybe not. But I'm sure he was forever plinking at all kinds of targets, moving and otherwise. Then, when it counted, David scored a bull's-eye.

"So," the Bible says matter-of-factly, "David triumphed over the Philistine with only a sling and a stone" (1 Samuel 17:50).

Is that all? Just a sling and a stone, and lots of practice? No, there was something more, something very important. David knew he couldn't clobber Goliath precisely in the forehead without God's help.

"I come to you," he told the dumbfounded giant, "in the name of the LORD of Heaven's Armies—the God of the armies of Israel, whom you have defied" (1 Samuel 17:45).

Goliath didn't have a chance!

Practice *and* trust—that's how to make bull's-eyes.

AUTHOR/CONTRIBUTOR BIOGRAPHIES

Joe Aldrich, Dr.—Past president of Multnomah University

Marziyeh Amirizadeh—Coauthor of *Captive in Iran*

Barry Arnold—Pastor, Cornerstone Church, Gresham, Oregon

Ramez Atallah—Director of Egyptian Bible Society and author of *How I Wish I Could Have Been There*

David Bradley—Name changed to protect the author

Oswald Chambers—Author of *My Utmost for His Highest* and other books; author of the article "O God, Make Thy Way Plain"

Stella Chan—Author of article *Open My Eyes, Lord!*

Frank Dietz—Author of article *In All Your Ways*

Alfy Franks—Author of *King of Hearts*

Bill Freeman—Editor of *How They Found Christ*

Bob Griffin—Missionary pilot and author of *Cleared for Takeoff*

Stephen Hart—Author of article *A President Paves the Way*

Carey Hauri—Author of *Walking Through the Night*

Don Hillis—Author of *When Contacts Matter*

Brenda Jacobson—Author of *Narrow Escape*

Tim Jennings—Author of *Prayer That Moves a Minivan*

David Jeremiah—Radio Broadcaster of *Turning Point* and author of many books

JESUS *Film*—www.jesusfilm.org

Paul H. Johnson—Real estate developer; author of *My Cup Runneth Over*; served on the boards of Moody Bible Institute, Christian Business Men's National Committee, Maranatha Bible Conference, Walk Thru the Bible, Winona Lake Conference, as well as others

Terri Justice—Author of *Bend Down, O Lord*

W. Phillip Keller—Author of many bestselling books

Greg Kernaghan—Author of *God Is Enough*

Carl Lawrence—Former director of Haven of Rest Ministries; the Gold Medallion winner for *The Coming Influence of China.* He served twenty years with Far East Broadcasting Company.

Beniamin Lup—European director of World Teach/Walk Thru the Bible

Tom Lyman—Author of *Manobo Girl Delivered from Demons*

Bernie May—Author of *What Counts Most?*

Josh McDowell—Author of *More Than a Carpenter*

Debbie Meroff—Author of *The Touch of the Master*

Dr. Helen Roseveare, M.D.—Missionary doctor in Zaire for twenty years

Doug Ross—President and CEO of Evangelical Christian Publishers Association from 1987 to 2004

Maryam Rostampour—Coauthor of *Captive in Iran*

Eric Schenkel—Executive director of *The* JESUS *Film Project*

John Van Diest—Book publisher for more than forty years and author/compiler of more than a dozen books

Pam Vredevelt—Counselor, popular speaker, and bestselling author

Bruce Wilkinson—Author of several books, including the bestselling *The Prayer of Jabez*

Dick Woodward—Megachurch quadriplegic pastor and inspirational speaker

Philip Yancey—Editor-at-large for *Christianity Today* and an author of eight Gold Medallion Award books

NOTES

MIRACLES OF DESTINY

People Love Secrets—Used by permission of International Cooperating Ministries from *4 Spiritual Secrets* by Dick Woodward.

Church Bells in the Kremlin—Used by permission of the author from *Praying with the KGB*, Philip Yancey, Multnomah Press, 1992.

Miracle of the Moscow Project—Used by permission of Doug Ross.

God at Work in Iraq—Used by permission of Ruth Aldrich.

The People Key—Rewritten by John Van Diest with permission of Bruce Wilkinson.

Five Fruitful Years—Used by permission of author from *My Cup Runneth Over*, Paul H. Johnson, 2013.

God Has Erased My Heart—Used by permission of author from *Cleared for Takeoff*, Bob Griffin, Harvest Day Books.

Martin Luther: A Troubled Conscience—Used by permission from *How They Found Christ*, Bill Freeman, ed.

How I Wish He Could Have Been There—Used by permission of the author, Ramez Atallah.

Triad and the Christian Book Fair—Used by permission of John Van Diest.

MIRACLES OF PRAYER

Burning Bush and Holy Moses—Used by permission of International Cooperating Ministries from *4 Spiritual Secrets*, by Dick Woodward.

Somebody Was Praying—Used by permission of the author from *Cleared for Takeoff*, Bob Griffin, Harvest Day Books.

Praying with the KGB—Used by permission of Philip Yancey.

Silhouette on the Screen—Used by permission from *The Power of JESUS*, wwwjesusfilm.org.

O God, Make Thy Way Plain—Used by permission of Discovery House Publishers, Grand Rapids, MI 49501 from *Oswald Chambers: Abandoned to God*, © 1993 by the Oswald Chambers Publications Assn., Ltd. All rights reserved.

What Counts Most?—Used by permission of the author, from *Under His Wing*, Bernie May, Multnomah Press.

Prayer That Moves a Minivan—Used by permission of the author, Tim Jennings.

The Prayers of an Old Lady—This story was told to John Van Diest, March 1, 2009.

An Ax Head Swim?—Used by permission of the author from *Cleared for Takeoff*, Bob Griffin, Harvest Day Books.

Rice Paddies Make Terrible Airstrips—Used by permission of the author from *Cleared for Takeoff*, Bob Griffin, Harvest Day Books.

Aurelius Augustine: A Sinful Life—Used by permission from *How They Found Christ* by Bill Freeman, ed.

MIRACLES OF PROTECTION

Captive in Iran—Used by permission from *Captive in Iran* by Maryam Rostampour & Marziyeh Amirizadeh, 2013, Tyndale House Publishers, Inc. All rights reserved.

Narrow Escape—Used by permission of author, Brenda Jacobson.

A Father's Heart—Used by permission, *The Touch of the Master*, 1996.

A Hug to End All Hugs—Used by permission of the author from *Cleared for Takeoff,* Bob Griffin, Harvest Day Books.

Under Fire—Used by permission, *The Touch of the Master,* 1996.

Typhoon!—Used by permission, *The Touch of the Master,* 1996.

Arrested in the Ivory Coast—Used by permission of John Van Diest.

Walking Through the Night—Used by permission, *The Touch of the Master,* 1996.

What Happened on March 9?—Rewritten by John Van Diest from *Prayer Adventure* by David Jeremiah.

Prisoners, and Yet...—Used by permission, *The Touch of the Master,* 1996.

MIRACLES OF PROVISION

Fresh Water—Used by permission of the author, Barry Arnold.

Fishing in China—Used by permission of the author from *The Coming Influence of China,* Carl Lawrence, Multnomah Books, 1996, p. 58.

The Bill Has Been Paid—Used by permission from *God, You and That Man with Three Goats!* by Don and Vera Hillis, self published, 1995.

The Well and the Wood—Anonymous. Gospel Gleaners, Springfield, Missouri, June 14, 1942. All evidence of the source of this miracle story is obscure since the organization has ceased.

More Company for Dinner!—Used by permission from *Splendour from the Sea* by W. Phillip Keller, Moody Publishers, 1979.

John Calvin: An Arrested Life—Used by permission from *How They Found Christ,* Bill Freeman, ed.

Jonathan Edwards: A Miserable Seeking—Used by permission from *How They Found Christ,* Bill Freeman, ed., pp. 79-80.

Sealed in Safety—Used by permission from *The Power of* JESUS of the *Jesus* Film Project, www.jesusfilm.org.

Before You Call, I Will Answer You—Used by permission of the author from *My Cup Runneth Over,* Paul H. Johnson.

In All Your Ways—Used by permission from *The Touch of the Master,* 1996.

Peter Rocks—Used by permission of International Cooperating Ministries from *4 Spiritual Secrets,* by Dick Woodward.

MIRACLES OF THE POWER OF JESUS

Rebelados—Used by permission from *The Power* of JESUS of the *Jesus* Film Project, www.jesusfilm.org.

A Special Kind of Love—Taken from *More Than a Carpenter* by Josh McDowell, 1977, 2005, used by permission Tyndale House Publishers, Inc. All rights reserved.

The Man in the Clouds—Used by permission from *The Power* of JESUS of the *Jesus* Film Project, www.jesusfilm.org.

An End Which Was a Beginning—Used by permission from *The Power* of JESUS of the *Jesus* Film Project, www.jesusfilm.org.

Manobo Girl Delivered from Demons—Used by permission of Tom Lyman.

700 Terrorists on the Ground—Used by permission from *The Power* of JESUS of the *Jesus* Film Project, www.jesusfilm.org.

The Strange Exchange—Used by permission of International Cooperating Ministries from *4 Spiritual Secrets* by Dick Woodward.

SIMPLE MIRACLES

Kicking the Habit—Used by permission of author John Van Diest.

We Have Been Waiting for You!—Used by permission from *The Power of* JESUS of the *Jesus* Film Project, www.jesusfilm.org.

Charles Spurgeon: A Seeking Heart—Used by permission from *How They Found Christ*, Bill Freeman, ed.

Taking Time Out—Used by permission of the author from *My Cup Runneth Over*, Paul H. Johnson.

You Are the Ones! You Are the Ones!—Used by permission from *The Power of* JESUS of the *Jesus* Film Project, www.jesusfilm.org.

A President Paves the Way—Used by permission from *The Touch of the Master*, 1996.

Just a Jackass—Used by permission of International Cooperating Ministries from *4 Spiritual Secrets* by Dick Woodward.

MIRACLES OF HEALING

Bend Down, O Lord—Used by permission from *Kindred Spirit* 32, Dallas Theological Seminary, 2008, p. 14.

God Is Enough—Used by permission from *The Touch of the Master*, 1996.

You Matter: A Message from Nathan—Used by permission of Pam Vredevelt.

Precious Seed—Used by permission from *The Touch of the Master*, 1996.

A Miracle-Working Church—Used by permission of the author from *The Coming Influence of China*, Carl Lawrence, Multnomah Press, 1996.

King of Hearts—Used by permission from *The Touch of the Master*, 1996.

Open My Eyes, Lord!—Used by permission from *The Touch of the Master*, 1996.

EVERYDAY MIRACLES

The Mountains of Iran—Used by permission of Ruth Aldrich.

Are You an Angel?— Used by permission of Bruce Wilkinson, rewritten by John Van Diest.

Hannah W. Smith—Used by permission of the author from *How They Found Christ*, Bill Freeman, ed.

When Contacts Matter—Used by permission from *God, You and That Man with Three Goats!*, Don W. Hillis (past president of the Evangelical Alliance Mission), p. 47.

A Korean Houseboy—Used by permission of the author from *My Cup Runneth Over*, Paul H. Johnson.

Bull's Eyes!—Used by permission of the author, Bob Griffin, missionary pilot.

ABOUT THE COMPILER

John Van Diest, a book publisher for more than 40 years, has played a key role in expanding Christian publishing around the globe. He is an accomplished author and the co-compiler of the bestselling Lists to Live By series and the coauthor of *The Secrets God Kept*. John lives with his wife, Pat, in Oregon.

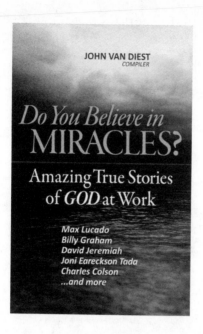

Do You Believe in Miracles?

Few things show God's amazing love and power like a miracle. *Do You Believe in Miracles?* is an extraordinary gathering of uplifting stories that reveal how God works through people and life events in surprising ways.

Whether you're a believer or just someone who loves a well-told story, you'll be inspired by these true tales of healing, answered prayer, and transformed lives. This hope-filled collection includes contributions from such well-known contributors as Billy Graham, Max Lucado, James Dobson, Chuck Colson, and Joni Eareckson Tada.

Read this book and discover wonder and inspiration in story after story that will fill you with the hope and assurance that God is active in the world and in your life today.

To learn more about Harvest House books and
to read sample chapters, visit our website:

www.harvesthousepublishers.com

HARVEST HOUSE PUBLISHERS
EUGENE, OREGON